About the Author

Educated at Columbia U worked as a journalist for up the *Wall Street Journal*'s first bureau in Beijing in 1979. Later, after nine years on the *Far Eastern Economic Review*, he moved to the *South China Morning Post* as Senior Columnist. He hosted the weekly current affairs TV programme *Newsline* on the World channel of Asia Television for twelve years. He lives in Hong Kong.

CHINA

The Truth About Its Human Rights Record

Frank Ching

RIDER

LONDON · SYDNEY · AUCKLAND · JOHANNESBURG

1 3 5 7 9 10 8 6 4 2

Published in 2008 by Rider, an imprint of Ebury Publishing
A Random House Group Company

The Random House Group Limited Reg. No. 954009

Addresses for companies within the Random House Group
can be found at
www.rbooks.co.uk

A CIP catalogue record for this book is available from
the British Library

The Random House Group Limited supports The Forest
Stewardship Council (FSC), the leading international forest
certification organisation. All our titles that are printed on Greenpeace
approved FSC certified paper carry the FSC logo.
Our paper procurement policy can be found at
www.rbooks.co.uk/environment

Printed and bound in Great Britain by CPI Cox & Wyman Ltd,
Reading, Berkshire

ISBN 978-1-84-604138-9

To buy books by your favourite authors and register for offers visit
www.rbooks.co.uk

Contents

Introduction

Amnesty International puts China in its list of twenty worst offenders of human rights in the world. Britain's *Observer* newspaper ranks China's human rights performance as the ninth worst. Human Rights Watch, in its 2008 report, says the Chinese Government 'continues to deny or restrict its citizens' fundamental rights, including freedom of expression, freedom of association, and freedom of religion'. Just how bad is the situation in China?

The answer: it's bad, but it used to be much worse.

Consider these figures: in the first three years after the People's Republic of China was established in 1949, Mao Zedong's communists killed between 800,000 and 3 million people in a campaign against landlords, rich peasants and former Kuomintang officials. In the urban purges in the 1950s, another 1 million people died. The Great Leap Forward of 1958–60, which aimed to industrialise China, resulted in 30 million deaths, many from starvation. And the Cultural Revolution, which began in 1966 and lasted until Mao's death in 1976, exacted a toll estimated at between 400,000 and 3 million. The total number of those killed is estimated at between 45 million and 70 million.

We hear more about the Cultural Revolution because it is the most recent but also because, in that campaign, Chairman Mao Zedong turned against his own people so that the main victims were Communist Party members themselves, ranging all the way up to chief of state Liu Shaoqi and party secretary Deng Xiaoping.

Mao loved political campaigns, which he launched in an endless round of class struggles to maintain the Communist Party's purity. No one was immune. Everyone had to study Mao's latest speeches and writings. Children reported on their parents, and students denounced their teachers.

Ordinary people had no rights. They could not even make personal decisions because in an environment where everything was highly politicised, there was no room for privacy. The government – or rather, the party – made such decisions as where a person lived, what to study, what job he or she was assigned to after graduation, and occasionally even whom to marry. Not infrequently, husbands and wives were assigned to live and work in different cities on a permanent basis.

Chairman Mao was the Great Leader, Great Teacher, Great Supreme Commander, and Great Helmsman. He was worshipped as a god, his every word having the force of law. Adulation of the leader was such that one story tells of how, when a little boy tore a page out of a newspaper to make a paper aeroplane, he was arrested and questioned for hours to determine if his parents had urged him to commit the grievous crime of desecrating the image of the Great Leader whose picture was printed on the page.

Political campaigns – against former landlords, rich peasants, counter-revolutionaries, bad elements, rightists and others not in political favour – filled the newspapers and the airwaves and everyone was expected to participate actively in denouncing those the state picked as targets, including colleagues, neighbours and even relatives.

There was no private business. There was little choice of what to eat and what to wear as the most basic things were rationed, such as grain, cooking oil, pork, coal, soap, eggs, sugar and cotton. Even after Deng Xiaoping turned the country around in 1978 and abandoned class struggle for economic development, old habits died hard and for a long time handbags made for export came in different designs and colours while those for domestic consumption were in just one colour: black.

That was China in the old days. And, during that time, almost no one in the West said a word about the lack of human rights in the country. Even Jimmy Carter, the human rights president who established diplomatic relations between the US and China, said not a word because Beijing was seen as a vital ally in the confrontation with the Soviet Union. Politics trumped human rights.

Mao's death eventually led to the new leader Deng Xiaoping deciding to end this total politicisation of society. Deng decided to focus the nation's energy on economic development and abandoned Mao's obsession with class struggle and world revolution. Since then, Deng and his successors have wrought an economic miracle.

Now, the command economy has been dismantled. The private sector has blossomed. While in the early days the private economy consisted of little more than individuals selling cups of tea on the street or turning their own homes into restaurants, today China has more billionaires in the world than any other country, second only to the United States.[1]

Today, life is very different. The rationing system is gone. Gone, too, is cradle-to-the-grave care by the government as people now struggle with things such as financing healthcare and pensions. China looks and feels much more like a normal country.

The cities are gleaming with brand-new glass and steel structures and the whole country has become one large construction site. Most people's standard of living has gone up to levels they could not possibly have imagined a few decades ago. Millions of people have been lifted from poverty.

China today is an economic superpower, with the fourth largest economy. Growth has been dazzling, with per capita gross domestic product (GDP) having increased from US$226 in 1978 to US$2,100. China–UK trade, which was less than US$1 billion in 1978, jumped to US$39.4 billion in 2007, nearly a forty-fold increase.[2]

That said, it must be kept in mind that China is a vast country and no one, not even the government, knows exactly who is doing what to whom in human rights terms. In 2007, stories emerged to the effect that hundreds, possibly thousands, of people – including children – had been kidnapped and forced to work as slaves in illegal kilns making bricks.

Then, in spring 2008, it was reported that some of the 'rescued' slaves had been resold back to different factories by local police and government officials. It is impossible to tell how extensive the problem of slave workers remains. With the state anxious to maintain its image both internationally and domestically and with the party's Propaganda Department constantly issuing directives to the media on what can and cannot be reported on, it is impossible to know the truth with any degree of certainty.

But despite China's acknowledged status as an economic superpower, it has not been included in the

Group of Eight advanced economies, which includes the United States, Japan, Germany, Britain, France, Canada, Italy and Russia, largely because the country is not a democracy and has a poor human rights record.

The Chinese Government, when challenged on its human rights performance, often responds that human rights have never been better in China and, as far as it goes, the statement is true. The government has withdrawn from vast areas of people's private lives but, in the political realm, the Communist Party will not stand for any opposition, especially organised opposition. And many journalists and lawyers have been thrown in prison for simply trying to stand up for their own rights or the rights of others.

But, at least, there are now journalists who dare to tell the truth – some of whom get thrown in prison for their efforts – and civil rights lawyers who are brave enough to defend them. And, while the legal system is far from perfect, today there are laws, and courts, and even the constitution was amended in 2004 to say: 'The state respects and preserves human rights.'

There were two factors that caused China's human rights record to be brought to the forefront, to be examined and denounced by Western nations. One was the disso-lution of the Soviet Union and the fall of communism in Eastern Europe. The second was the Tiananmen Square massacre of 4 June 1989. The two in fact were linked.

Just as a common fear of the Soviet Union brought the United States and China together, so the disappearance of the Soviet threat meant that China was no longer that important to Washington. In fact, Mikhail Gorbachev's historic visit to Beijing in May 1989 was to signal the end of decades of Sino–Soviet hostility. The world's press descended on Beijing to cover this historic event only to discover that there was an even bigger story brewing in Tiananmen Square: the massive demonstrations triggered by the death of Hu Yaobang on 15 April that resulted in calls for political reforms, democracy, a free press and an end to corruption. The students' creation of a 10-metre high Goddess of Democracy patterned after the Statue of Liberty in New York harbour underlined the liberal values that they espoused.

Because of the presence of the world's media, people around the world saw horrific pictures of Chinese troops pouring into Beijing and crushing the unarmed demonstrators. These pictures were sent into living rooms in Washington, London and Paris and other major cities. The West responded with economic sanctions and ostracism as well as an embargo on the sale of weapons.

China argues that such an embargo is a relic of the Cold War and should be lifted. The Chinese Government insists that there is nothing to fear from China's 'peaceful rise', but the rest of the world is unconvinced that China will not change its tune after it becomes a political and military superpower and not just an economic one. That is a major factor why the countries of the West want to see China transformed into a democracy, embracing the same values that they espouse, including, of course, the cherishing of human rights.

Currently, China remains a single-party state, and the country's constitution specifies that it is under the leadership of the Communist Party. Chinese leaders frequently say that it is their intention to move towards greater democracy, human rights and rule of law, but they do not want to move too quickly for fear of political destabilisation.

However, while democracy remains a distant dream for those who fight for civil rights, the atmosphere today is already strikingly different from thirty years ago, when people were fearful of speaking their minds. Nowadays taxi drivers are quick to let you know what they think of the government. Newspapers, though still controlled, are much more varied. A wide range of magazines and books are being published and even stores featuring sex toys function openly in a society that was until recently quite puritanical.

China's decision to move glacially, if at all, on political reform is very much a result of what happened to the former Soviet Union which, under Gorbachev, decided on *glasnost*, or political reforms, before *perestroika,* or economic reforms, with results that are all too visible. To China, that is something to be avoided at all costs.

But that doesn't mean there has been no political

change. Under Mao, political leaders served for life, and both Mao and his right-hand man, Premier Zhou Enlai, held office until the day they died. Now, the revolutionary concept of term limits has been introduced, as well as set retirement age for various posts.

Former President Jiang Zemin stepped down as party leader in 2002 and as head of state in 2003 to observe a two-term limit on those offices. The current leader, Hu Jintao, will have to do the same thing in 2012 and 2013, after serving two five-year terms. This looks likely to continue indefinitely, with the leader, whoever it is, being in power for no more than ten years.

As for elections, democratic elections at grassroots level have been introduced, and village heads are now elected by the villagers themselves. Party leaders promise that eventually elections will be held at township level, then at province level and then at national level. However, the process seems inordinately slow.

China has been excoriated for its human rights record by the West, especially the United States. In response, China now issues an annual human rights report on the United States, in retaliation for American reports each year on China and on practically every other country in the world – except for the United States itself.

But the two are talking past each other. Their idea of human rights is different.

The United Nations General Assembly in 1968 approved two conventions on human rights: the International Covenant on Civil and Political Rights and the International Covenant on Economic, Social and Cultural Rights. These expand upon the rights that are included in the Universal Declaration of Human Rights.

Interestingly, the United States ratified the ICCPR in 1994, fifteen years after signing it, but it has never ratified the ICESCR. China, on the other hand, has ratified the ICESCR but has not yet ratified the ICCPR, which it signed in 1998.[3]

Not surprisingly, American human rights reports focus narrowly on civil and political rights, such as the right to vote, in particular the right to change the government through elections, and the upholding of such rights as the freedom of the press, freedom of expression, freedom from torture, freedom from arbitrary deprivation of life and so on.

China, on the other hand, gives priority to economic rights, in particular the right to subsistence. China, along with some other developing countries, feels that the responsibility to feed and clothe its people must come first, and any political rights can only follow after a country or society has reached a certain level of development.

Thus, the United States depicts China as 'an authoritarian state in which . . . the Communist Party is the paramount source of power.'

And China describes the United States as 'a violent,

crime-ridden society with a severe infringement of the people's rights by law enforcement departments and with a lack of guarantee for the life of the people, their freedom and personal safety'.

While the US talks about Chinese governmental actions that result in the curtailment of human rights, China responds by focusing on such things as crime and violence, even though these are not perpetrated by the government. However, from the standpoint of the victim, the fact that he is executed by the government or killed in a shooting rampage by a crazed gunman makes little difference. He is just as dead, and his right to life was not protected.

China's insistence on economic rights before political rights is shared by developing countries in general. This became clear in April 1993, when the first Asian conference on human rights was held in Bangkok. Then Thai prime minister, Chuan Leekpai, in his opening address, declared that while human rights were universal, the path towards realising the Universal Declaration of Human Rights 'lies through economic development, democratisation and social justice'. He added: 'I cannot stress enough the importance of the right of the peoples and nations in Asia, as elsewhere in the world, to develop.'

From a historical standpoint, it is true to say that the Universal Declaration adopted by the United Nations in 1948 was largely drafted by the developed countries of the

West and reflected their social, political and cultural values. They probably did not consider the right to development, for example, as important because they were already developed.

Also, while a free press might be considered a key right in developed countries, it may be less meaningful in a society with a high degree of illiteracy.[4] But when a society's economic development is such that most people can read and write, then it is in a much better position to practise such rights as freedom of speech and freedom of the press. The link between economic development – that is, economic rights – and political rights should be obvious.

So it is not surprising that the Bangkok Declaration, adopted on 2 April 1993, asserted the right to economic development as 'a universal and inalienable right and an integral part of fundamental human rights'. That right was not in the Universal Declaration but has since then been embraced by the developing countries of Asia, Africa and Latin America in regional human rights conferences.

Moreover, many people in Asia find it perplexing that in the West there seems to be no linkage between rights and responsibilities. There is a feeling that a mature society should inculcate in its people not only a sense of respect for the rights of others but also for each person to have a sense of responsibility. Many see the widespread violence and crime in major American cities as a sign that the United

States has gone too far in protecting the rights of individuals without safeguarding the rights of society as a whole.

The Universal Declaration says: 'Everyone has the right to life, liberty and the security of person.' Human rights organisations invoke this almost always to restrain the hand of government. But it can be argued that anyone who lives in a crime-ridden city where it is unsafe to venture outdoors after dark is being deprived of the exercise of his liberty. It matters little whether a person's rights are being infringed by the government or by others. A person's right to security should include the right not to be mugged, robbed, raped, murdered, accosted, assaulted, humiliated or intimidated on the streets, sometimes in broad daylight. Keeping the streets safe is part of a government's responsibility to uphold the human rights of its citizens. But this point of view is rarely if ever voiced by Western governments or human rights organisations.

China's growing prosperity has made life more complicated for many. There has been a general rise in prosperity but also increasing polarisation between the haves and the have-nots. A new class of people has emerged, migrant workers, mostly men from the countryside who work on construction sites and women who toil away in factories making toys, clothing or decorations for Western markets. Many are taken advantage of by their employers, who often underpay them and sometimes refuse to pay at all.

Land has also become scarce with farmland being converted into housing, shopping malls, roads etc. In the process, many officials enrich themselves while farmers are thrown off the land that they had worked with little compensation.

This has resulted in massive protests, some of them well publicised. There are tens of thousands of huge protests each year. Local authorities, of course, try to clamp down on journalists who seek information as well as on lawyers who try to provide legal assistance to those victimised or arrested for staging demonstrations. This is a fertile field for human rights abuses. There have been horrific tales of abuse of power as well as inspiring stories of individuals who are willing to stand up to the rich and powerful on behalf of vulnerable farmers, often at risk of physical assault, imprisonment or worse.

Thus, the human rights story in China is a mixed one. On one hand, there continues to be egregious violations; on the other, there are indications that things are getting better, though perhaps not quickly enough. We will be discussing both the pluses and the minuses in the following chapters.

1.

Law and Order

In late 2005, China allowed Manfred Nowak, the United Nations rapporteur on torture, to visit the country and inspect its prisons to fulfil its obligation as a signatory to the Convention Against Torture and Other Cruel, Inhuman or Degrading Treatment or Punishment. Unfortunately for Beijing, Mr Nowak concluded that 'the practice of torture, though on the decline – particularly in the urban areas – remains widespread in China'. Mr Nowak reported that 'some government authorities, particularly the Ministries of State Security and Public Security, attempted at various times throughout the visit to obstruct or restrict' his attempts at fact-finding.

Mr Nowak commented that the Chinese legal system as it existed was an obstacle to combating torture because there was

an absence of essential procedural safeguards necessary to make its prohibition effective,

including the effective exclusion of evidence from
statements established to be made as a result of
torture: the presumption of innocence; the privilege
against self-incrimination; timely notice of reasons
for detention or arrest; prompt external review of
detention or arrest; granting of non-custodial
measures, such as bail; the right of habeas corpus;
and timely access to counsel and adequate time
and facilities to prepare a defence.

He urged China to reform its criminal procedure law to
provide for the right to remain silent and the privilege against
self-incrimination, the right to cross-examine witnesses
and the effective exclusion of evidence extracted through
torture. Mr Nowak urged that China allow lawyers, particularly criminal defence lawyers, 'to be more effective in
representing the rights and interest of their clients including
through involvement at the earliest stage of policy custody
and pre-trial detention'.

One big problem is that while the state says that it
does not condone torture, the courts continue to accept
evidence extracted through torture. This was evident in a
number of cases where the defendant confessed to crimes
that he did not commit, including murder. The government
was red-faced when the wife of She Xianglin, a former
security guard who was executed in 2005 for her murder,

turned up very much alive later that year. The man had confessed to her murder under torture after the police identified a body as that of his wife. It turned out that she had run away to another province, married another man and had been totally unaware of the murder charge.

Angry and embarrassed by Mr Nowak's charges, the government did take some action. China's top prosecutor, Jia Chunwang, president of the Supreme People's Procuratorate, announced in 2006 that in a bid to enhance the judicial protection of human rights, the procuratorate had launched special campaigns to crack down on human rights infringement cases committed by government officials.

He acknowledged that extracting confessions through torture by the police was a widespread practice. He said prosecutors had redressed 598 cases of such confessions or those in which evidence was obtained illegally. They had investigated a further 110 cases concerning forced confessions.

Such admissions of illegality by top judicial officials are rare, and underlined the seriousness of the problems confronting the mainland's criminal justice system.

Guilty Until Proven Innocent

Among steps taken by the procuratorate to protect the interests of suspects is the videotaping of interrogations of suspects in major cases. However, China's legal and judicial systems remain underdeveloped. One problem is the party's long-term policy of 'leniency to those who confess and severity to those who refuse to do so'. The assumption is that the suspect is guilty and that the only way out is to confess. Such an attitude is totally at odds with the West's idea of respecting the rights of a suspect, who is considered to be innocent until proven guilty.

To change ingrained attitudes, it would be necessary to reform the mentality of all police officers as well as those who work for the judiciary and the procuratorate to respect due process of law. There is also a need to put greater emphasis on evidence and less on confessions.

At present, there is no level playing field where suspects are concerned, as made clear by the US State Department in its 2008 report on human rights in China:

> Public security organs do not require court-approved warrants to detain suspects under their administrative detention powers. After detention the procuracy can approve formal arrest without court approval. According to the law, in routine criminal cases police can unilaterally detain persons for up to 37 days before releasing them or formally placing them under arrest. After a suspect is arrested, the law allows police and prosecutors to detain a person for up to seven months while public security organs further investigate the case.

Another one and one-half months of detention are allowed where public security organs refer a case to the procuratorate to decide whether to file charges. If charges are filed, authorities can detain a suspect for an additional one and one-half month period between filing and trial. However, in practice the police sometimes detained persons beyond the time limits stipulated by law.[1]

Moreover, the vague wording of legislation and imprecise definitions of crimes leave much room for discretion for the law enforcement and prosecution authorities. Crimes such as 'endangering national security', 'disrupting social order' or 'subverting public order' are so vague that it is difficult to disprove the charges.

One unique Chinese legal institution is called 'Re-education Through Labour' under which people can be sentenced by the police to prison terms without charge, trial or judicial review. These sentences are decided administratively rather than judicially and can be used to intimidate political activists. The sentences can also be extended at the whim of the authorities.

Mr Nowak called for an end to other practices, such as 'forced re-education of detainees in prisons and pre-trial detention centres and psychiatric hospitals'.

The Judiciary, Laws and Lawyers

A weak link in the Chinese criminal justice system is the judiciary. The system was basically rebuilt from scratch in the 1970s but with a severe shortage of legally trained officials, people with a security background such as police service were assigned to work as judges. In the 1990s, it was common for retired military officers with no judicial background to be appointed as judges. Today, at least all judges have to pass the national bar examination.

Another big problem with judges in China is that they are treated and paid like government officials, with their salaries coming from the budgets of local and provincial governments. That in effect takes away their independence and, in cases involving the government, judges almost always come down on the side of their employer. A centralised system of payment, with all judges in the country being paid out of the judiciary's national budget, should go a long way toward resolving the problem of judicial local protectionism.

One encouraging development is the emergence in China of a corps of dedicated lawyers who are committed to upholding civil rights. They are known as *weiquan* lawyers, or lawyers who uphold civil rights, and sometimes simply as human rights defenders.

But the government has many instruments at its disposal to put pressure on such lawyers, including beating them up, cancelling their registration certificates as lawyers and, in extreme cases, throwing them in prison. Some have been subjected to long periods of arbitrary detention without charge. Others have been set upon by thugs, apparently at the instigation of the police. Almost all are kept under constant surveillance. Their families, too, are subjected to pressure and are easily targeted.

New regulations have been drafted to restrict the ability of lawyers to represent groups of victims and to participate in collective petitions. For example, the practice certificate of Gao Zhisheng, an outspoken human rights lawyer, was suspended in November 2005. The following August he was detained and was held incommunicado until his trial in December 2006. It was not until October 2007 that he was formally arrested on charges of 'inciting subversion' and in December 2007 he was sentenced to three years in prison – a sentence that was suspended for five years. This means that in the five-year period, the sentence can be applied any time he steps out of line.

The former Shanghai lawyer Zheng Enchong's licence was revoked and he was sentenced to three years in 2003 for 'illegally providing state secrets abroad' because of two faxes that he allegedly sent to the New York-based organisation Human Rights in China. He had helped hundreds of victims of forced eviction stemming from urban redevelopment in Shanghai and apparently sent relevant information to international organisations.

Legal Activist Chen Guangcheng

Chen Guangcheng is a self-taught lawyer who has been blind since childhood. He became a celebrity because he was the first to champion the cause of other disabled people who had been victims of discrimination. He then went further and tried to bring a class action lawsuit against the local government in Shandong province for carrying out a campaign of forced abortion and sterilisation to meet birth control quotas.

Local officials in Linyi city, Shandong province, were embarrassed. In June 2006, he was charged with damaging property and organising a mob to disrupt traffic.

Lawyers flocked to defend him. And yet, just before his trial, three members of his legal team were arrested for alleged theft. When other members of his legal team asked for a postponement, the judge refused, instead appointing two lawyers to represent him with whom he had never discussed the case. Those lawyers did not object to any of the prosecution's allegations and did not call any witnesses in his defence.

Mr Chen himself protested against these proceedings by refusing to take part. The judge declared that his silence amounted to an admission of guilt. (In China, the law does not recognise a right to silence.)[2]

It is not clear how a blind person could have been guilty of organising the damage of property and directing the obstruction of traffic – especially at a time when he was under close police supervision.

Moreover, even assuming he did damage 'doors and windows' as well as cars and interrupted traffic for three hours, it is difficult to argue that a four-year prison sentence is somehow proportionate to the offence. The whole episode was a travesty of justice.

Because of his 'irrepressible passion for justice in leading ordinary citizens to assert their legitimate rights under the law', he was given the 2007 Ramon Magsaysay Award for Emergent Leadership.

As Chen was in prison, his wife, Yuan Weijing, decided to fly to Manila to accept the award on his behalf. However, she was stopped from boarding the plane, apparently by police from the Linyi region of Shandong province, where she lived. The police also confiscated her passport without providing any reason for denying her right to travel.

On 6 March 2008, another lawyer, thirty-four-year-old Teng Biao, disappeared. His wife, Wang Ling, said that he had been bundled into a black car with no number plate – a clear indication of the work of the public security bureau. Teng had been part of a network of activists who have used test cases, online petitions and other methods to campaign for the strengthening of civil rights.

Before his disappearance, Teng had urged the authorities to release Hu Jia, an outspoken dissident in Beijing who was snatched from his home in December 2007 and on 3 April 2008 was sentenced to three and a half years in prison on charges of inciting subversion. Teng has called for the ending of the *hukou*, or residence permit, system which limits the rights of millions of migrant workers.

Surprisingly, Teng was released after two days by the police, who never admitted that they were holding him. Teng said he had been questioned sternly and that public security officers warned him about recent articles he had posted on the Internet.

Teng's abduction by the police may well be connected to the case of Hu Jia. The two men had jointly signed a petition, titled 'The Real China Before the Olympics'. (A summary of this petition is given in an appendix at the end of this book.)

The Basic Principles on the Role of Lawyers, adopted by the United Nations General Assembly in 1990, state: 'Governments shall recognise and respect that all communications and consultations between lawyers and their clients within their professional relationship are confidential.' The principles also stipulate that governments have the duty to ensure that lawyers can fulfil their functions without fear of harassment or improper interference.

Another United Nations principle states: 'All arrested, detained or imprisoned persons shall be provided with adequate opportunities, time and facilities to be visited by and to communicate and consult with a lawyer, without delay, interception or censorship and in full confidentiality.'

The Chinese Government likes to present itself as a responsible international citizen. It should no longer act in a manner that is clearly contrary to these United Nations principles. It cannot afford to flout such basic international norms as the right of accused persons to timely and confidential legal advice and the right of lawyers to represent their clients without being intimidated and harassed by the government or its hired thugs.

Despite the intimidation of lawyers, the Chinese authorities have from time to time also taken relatively progressive steps forward. Thus, in October 2007, the National People's Congress, China's parliament, amended the law on lawyers, giving lawyers legal rights that are taken for granted in other countries.

Under the amended law, defence lawyers will be able to meet their clients after police interrogation without having to apply for permission, and conversations between lawyers and clients will no longer be monitored by the police. Until the law came into effect in June 2008, lawyers needed police permission to meet their clients – permission that was not always granted.

Interestingly, the new law did not make an exception for cases involving state secrets – a nebulous and very elastic concept.[3] This created a conflict with the criminal procedure law, which specifies that approval to meet defendants is required in cases involving state secrets. Presumably, the criminal procedure law will have to be amended but that has not yet happened.

Under the new law, defence lawyers will be entitled to look at files and other materials relating to a case and to collect evidence on their own. They are also entitled to apply to prosecutors and the courts to seek relevant evidence, and to get witnesses to testify in court.

These may all sound like very basic rights for both lawyers and defendants, but in China, where the presumption of innocence does not exist, they are a substantial step forward.

In fact, as the official *China Daily* said, 'The role of lawyers to defend a criminal suspect has remained controversial for quite some time – because criminal suspects were not presumed to be innocent. Once a person was arrested, he or she would generally be considered a criminal even before being convicted.'[4]

However, the failure of the National People's Congress to amend the criminal procedure law creates much uncertainty, since a provision in that law provides that investigative authorities can turn down an application for a meeting between a lawyer and his client in custody, and that they can send someone to be present during the meeting.

State Secrets

As to just what a state secret is, Human Rights in China has this to say: 'The State Secrets Law and its Implementing Regulations provide a list of categories of what may be state secrets, but the lists are so broad and vague as to encompass essentially all conceivable information.'

Currently, things such as the number of drug addicts, of HIV/AIDS sufferers, of people executed each year, the seriousness of the unemployment problem, the frequency and seriousness of public protests, can all be considered state secrets. In addition, the strategy and overall plan of land use development, environmental quality reports, data on public health disasters caused by environmental pollution, information on serious accidents or industrial illnesses, unemployment and poverty of workers, and accusations against party leaders can all come under the rubric of state secrets.

But these are all issues that need to be confronted. Sweeping them under the carpet does not solve the problem and does not help China. Besides, the prevalence of secrets lends itself to abuse. Officials often make use of the charge of disclosing state secrets in order to keep a veil over their own mistakes.

Bizarrely, the fact that something is a secret can in itself also be a secret. Thus, some Chinese are in a catch-22 situation: they cannot tell the truth, nor can they explain why they cannot tell the truth.

These rights continue to be invoked by the police and the prosecution.

Because of the bias against defendants, defence lawyers were viewed as people who were trying to help criminals escape punishment. Thus, the system was loaded against defence lawyers in favour of prosecutors. The right to legal representation itself was questioned.

Lawyers, therefore, found their work extremely difficult. They were frequently not permitted to liaise with their clients and had no access to relevant files. This meant that they were frequently ineffective, and could do little more than ask the court for leniency.

While the amended legislation provides for immunity for statements made in court by lawyers, it also prohibits lawyers from expressing opinions that 'threaten state security, defame others and disturb court order'. Given China's notoriously wide definition of national security, this may serve to inhibit lawyers when they make statements.

The amendments, no doubt, represent an improvement for lawyers and their clients but they do not go nearly far enough. As Nicholas Bequelin of Human Rights Watch has pointed out, the original plan was to give bar associations greater self-regulatory powers. However, the amended law keeps bar associations firmly under the control of the Ministry of Justice.[5]

Moreover, a new clause has been introduced in the law

that reflects the authorities' concerns about legal activism. It specifically prohibits lawyers from 'inciting and instigating plaintiffs to adopt illegal means such as creating public disturbances and harming public order to solve disputes'.

The revised law came a year and a half after new curbs on lawyers issued by the All China Lawyers Association (ACLA) on the handling of mass cases.

In March 2006, the ACLA issued 'Guiding Opinions' for lawyers who represent protesters and plaintiffs bringing collective lawsuits. Among other things, lawyers were called on to provide confidential information that they had learned from their clients to the authorities. This was most disturbing because, very often, the authorities were the ones that the plaintiffs were taking action against.

The 'Guiding Opinions' also instructed lawyers to seek 'supervision and guidance' of judicial administrative bureaux when handling mass cases involving ten or more plaintiffs. The judicial bureaux are part of local governments so that consulting them is, in effect, consulting the local governments whom farmers accuse of confiscating their land with little or no compensation in order to make deals with developers.

But the revised lawyers' law has raised hope for more positive changes, including the possible acceptance by China of the notion of presumption of innocence.

The Death Penalty

Another recent reform was aimed at reducing the number of executions in the country. The exact number is not known, since it is considered a state secret, but it is known that China executes more people every year than the rest of the world combined.

The death penalty is applicable to around sixty-eight offences in the Chinese criminal law, including several violent crimes, such as robbery, rape and murder. It is also applicable to some 'white collar' crimes such as tax fraud and embezzlement, and drug offences where the circumstances are considered to be serious.

As a result of obviously innocent men being executed after confessions extracted through torture, as in the case of She Xianglin, the Supreme People's Court decided to review all cases of capital punishment throughout the country before the sentences were carried out.

Xiao Yang, then chief justice, announced that all reviews of death sentences would have to be heard in open court. Although the law already provided for public hearings, that provision was widely flouted.

By law, all death penalty cases have to be reviewed by a higher court. For twenty-three years, such reviews were routinely heard by provincial courts until the Supreme People's Court finally withdrew this power from provincial courts and vested it in special tribunals.

The death sentence was often upheld with little chance for the appellant to speak or to provide evidence. Now, the top court is telling judges to listen carefully to the reasons for an appeal, and to review the evidence.

The Rule of Law

The basic problem with China's legal system is that there is no culture of rule of law. Rather, the Communist Party is trying to make law its instrument of control. One example is the way the authorities have dealt with Zhao Yan, a *New York Times* researcher who was first detained in September 2004 and charged with leaking state secrets. The *New York Times* had published an article predicting, accurately, that former leader Jiang Zemin would step down as head of the Central Military Commission.

Zhao was picked up ten days later. Apparently Beijing believed that he had provided that information – considered a state secret – to the newspaper. Both the newspaper and Zhao denied the accusation. The Bush administration repeatedly called for Zhao's release. He was finally acquitted on the state secrets charge but convicted of fraud in an allegation unrelated to his employment at the newspaper. When the Chinese government makes up its mind to get someone, it seems, it can do so whether it is on one charge or another.

If China were to ratify the International Covenant on Civil

and Political Rights, which it signed a decade ago, and observe its provisions, it would go a long way towards having a respectable system of justice. But before that can happen, the Party has to decide that it will come under the law rather than be above it.

2.

A Question of Faith

Although the rulers of the People's Republic of China are communists and hence by definition atheists, every state constitution drafted since 1949 has included a provision for freedom of religion. In the 1982 constitution, which is the one currently in force, Article 36 stipulates:

Citizens of the People's Republic of China enjoy freedom of religious belief.

No state organ, public organisation or individual may compel citizens to believe in, or not to believe in, any religion; nor may they discriminate against citizens who believe in, or do not believe in, any religion.

The state protects normal religious activities. No one may use religion to engage in activities that disrupt public order, impair the health of citizens or interfere with the educational system of the state.

Religious bodies and religious affairs are not subject to any foreign domination.

Despite constitutional safeguards, however, the Chinese Government admits that religious believers had been subjected to severe persecution, especially in the Cultural Revolution. Thus, a paper, 'Freedom of Religious Belief in China', published by the Information Office of the State Council in October 1997, acknowledged: 'The "cultural revolution" (1966 to 1976) had a disastrous effect on all aspects of the society in China, including religion. But in the course of correcting the errors of the "cultural revolution" governments at all levels made great efforts to revive and implement the policy of freedom of religious belief, redressed the unjust, false or wrong cases imposed on religious personages, and reopened sites for religious activities.'

Communism and Religion

Ideology is extremely important to the Communist Party and it is a major concession for the communists to allow someone not to believe in communism. But, aside from conceding a right to believe in religion, the constitution does not allow missionary activity in China or proselytising so as to convert non-believers. In fact, giving children religious instruction is controversial although the Chinese Government acceded to a US request in 2003 that minors are entitled to religious education. Subsequently, however, it appeared that at least in the Xinjiang region, with a large Muslim population, religious education of minors remained a contentious issue.

Religion is also clearly seen as something that is dangerous, that may result in the disruption of public order, or impair the health of citizens, or interfere in the education of citizens, or even lead to foreign domination of China.

However, the Communist Party has in recent times looked with greater favour on religion, as it has emphasised the need for harmony in society. The Party traditionally was a vehicle for instilling not harmony but class hatred and class struggle as Mao launched one political campaign after another, pitting different groups against each other. But religion which teaches people to be patient, to forgive transgressors, to be tolerant, can do much to instil harmony in society.

There are five religions recognised by the state, namely Buddhism, Taoism, Islam, Catholicism and Protestantism. Interestingly, the number of religious believers has exploded in recent years as faith in communism has dropped. It is estimated that there are up to 200 million believers in a country of 1.3 billion people.

So it is perhaps not surprising that in March 2008, the

Communist Party changed its own charter to make room for the concept of religion in the pursuit of social harmony. It was the first time since the party was founded in 1921 that anything related to religion was incorporated into its charter. Moreover, Jia Qingling, fourth ranking party leader, said in a keynote address at the opening session of the National Committee of the Chinese People's Political Consultative Conference in March 2008: 'We should fully follow the policy on freedom of religious belief, implement the regulations on religious affairs, and conduct thorough research on important and difficult issues related to religion. We should guide religious leaders and believers to improve their lives and make full use of their positive role in promoting social harmony.'

Tibetan Buddhism

The communists see religion as something that needs to be controlled and that can be made use of. In Tibet, for example, the highly religious Tibetans are not permitted to honour their spiritual leader, the Dalai Lama, who lives in exile in India. Increasingly, China is trying to control Tibetan religious leaders, including the second-ranking Panchen Lama and other Living Buddhas.

In summer 2007, China took the unusual step of announcing new regulations governing Tibetan Buddhism, including a stipulation that senior monks, known as 'living

Buddhas', cannot be reincarnated without government permission. Thus, the secular state is not only intruding into religious affairs but actually arrogating to itself the authority to decide when and whether a 'living Buddha' can be reincarnated – clearly a religious activity.

These regulations obviously have implications for the present Dalai Lama, who is now seventy-two years old and lives in exile in India, beyond China's control. The Chinese Government wants to change this situation. It does not relish the idea of having to deal with another potential opposition figure if the Dalai Lama should be reincarnated among Tibetan exiles. But if it can determine that the Dalai Lama is reincarnated within China, then it will be in a position to control the education of the child and to groom him to become a 'patriotic' Dalai Lama willing to co-operate with the Communist Party.

Beijing accuses the present Dalai Lama of being a 'splittist' who advocates Tibetan independence even though the Dalai Lama himself says all he wants is true autonomy for Tibet within the Chinese nation. Not surprisingly, one article in the new regulations declares: 'Reincarnating living Buddhas should respect and protect the principles of the unification of the state . . .'

Traditionally, Tibet was a theocracy, with the Dalai Lama being both the spiritual and political head. Tibetans practise their own religion, speak their own language and have remained apart from Han Chinese. The region is rich in minerals and serves as a buffer with China's western and southern neighbours.

During the Cultural Revolution, it is estimated that Red Guards destroyed more than 90 per cent of the monasteries and other religious institutions. The late Chinese leader Hu Yaobang publicly apologised in Lhasa for thirty years of bad policies and ordered most Chinese officials there to be replaced by Tibetans.

In March 2008, violence broke out in Lhasa, the Tibetan capital, at the culmination of days of protests by Buddhist monks. Han Chinese shopkeepers were beaten up and, according to official Chinese sources, twenty-two people died, mostly as a result of being burned to death after their premises were set on fire. Tibetan exile sources said up to a hundred Tibetans had been killed, but there was no confirmation. Chinese officials, meanwhile, said not a single shot was fired and no lethal weapons had been used in quelling the Lhasa demonstrations although they admitted that some Tibetans in other areas were killed.

It was ironic that just as Beijing was planning to bask in the glow of international acceptance of a rising, peaceful China, the violence in Lhasa might result in the spotlight falling instead on a China that suppresses demonstrations by Tibetan monks, that cracks down on advocates of human rights and is associated with the world's most recalcitrant regimes.

Back in 2001, when Beijing won the bid to host the Olympic Games, there were rapturous celebrations in the country as it looked forward to finally regaining its proper place in the world. But after the Tibetan riots there was a danger that the Olympics would magnify the country's failings even more than its achievements.

Premier Wen Jiabao, at his annual press conference held at the end of the latest National People's Congress session on 18 March 2008, accused the 'Dalai clique' of having orchestrated the riots in order to sabotage the summer games. In Dharamsala, the Dalai Lama denied that he had incited violence and said the Chinese could examine all his files. He even threatened to resign if the situation in Tibet went out of control.

That raised an unprecedented situation. No Dalai Lama has ever resigned and, in theory, a new Dalai Lama cannot be chosen as the reincarnation until after the death of the old Dalai Lama.

The Chinese Government has been injecting money into the Tibetan economy, including the construction of a railway to link the region with major cities such as Shanghai and Beijing. The idea was that a rising standard of living would lessen Tibetan opposition to Chinese rule.

However, the attacks on Chinese businesses suggest that many Tibetans feel that only the new migrants, Han Chinese and Muslims, have benefited from the improving economy rather than the indigenous population.

There is actually no reason for Beijing to be fearful of Tibet's secession. No country in the world recognises the Tibetan government-in-exile and even India has reaffirmed its position that Tibet is part of China.

In 1959, after the Tibetan uprising that led to the flight of the Dalai Lama to India, Mao Zedong predicted that, in the twenty-first century, things would have changed so much that the Dalai Lama would want to return. Before that can happen, however, Mao's successors must first create the necessary conditions.

The new regulations on reincarnations make official something that has been China's position for years: the right of the Chinese government to make decisions for Tibetan Buddhists.

Beijing has defended its involvement in Tibetan religious affairs by citing precedents going back to the Yuan dynasty (1279–1368) of the Mongols and the Qing Dynasty (1644–1911) of the Manchus. The title 'living Buddha' was

The Panchen Lama

In 1995, the Dalai Lama designated a boy in Tibet as the reincarnation of the last Panchen Lama, who had died in 1989. But the Chinese Government picked a different boy and declared him the Panchen Lama's real reincarnation. There is no information available on the whereabouts of the Dalai Lama-designated boy.

first conferred on a Tibetan religious leader in the thirteenth century by Kublai Khan, the Mongol leader who founded the Yuan dynasty.

But there is a difference. The Mongols, who governed China during the Yuan dynasty, made Lamaist Buddhism the official religion and had the greatest respect for Tibetan religious leaders. Similarly, during the Manchu (Qing) dynasty, the emperor was a patron of the Dalai Lama.

While no doubt the religious activities of Mongol and Manchu rulers were to some extent a cloak for justifying their imperial ambitions, they did purport to uphold and revere the traditions and beliefs of their various subjects. The situation today, however, is one in which the Communist Party, whose state religion is atheism, cannot be seen as either a believer in Buddhism or a patron of the faith. It is simply the state extending its authority into religious affairs. This is similar to the current stand-off between China and the Vatican, where Beijing insists on its right to appoint bishops.

Ultimately, it all boils down to a matter of control. The Chinese Government is unwilling to share power, even over religious matters.

Christianity and the Church

To a large extent, the stricture against foreign domination of religion in the Chinese constitution was instituted for the benefit of the Roman Catholic Church.

This stems from the earliest days of the People's Republic. In 1950, less than a year after the founding of the new state, Chinese Protestants were encouraged to 'cast off imperialist influence' and achieve the goals of the 'Three Selfs' – self-administration, self-support and self-propagation of Chinese churches.

Catholics were told to cut off their relationship with 'imperialism in all aspects', that is including the Pope. The communists justified the severance of Chinese Christians from their fellow believers overseas by citing the role played by missionaries in the nineteenth century, some of whom were alleged to have worked closely with Western governments, including serving as guides, interpreters and information officers during attacks on China in 1900.

By the early 1950s, many bishops, priests and believers were arrested, some of whom died in jail. In 1955, a mass arrest took place in Shanghai with more than 200 arrests on 8 September, including Bishop Ignatius Kung, who refused to support the 'three self' movement.

The Vatican has refused to recognise the 'patriotic' Chinese church and Catholics who maintained their loyalty to Rome went underground, worshipping in private homes rather than in the state-recognised churches where the 'patriotic' Catholics worshipped. To this day, Catholics in China are divided between the 'patriotic' and the 'underground' churches.

This has proved a severe impediment to the establishment of diplomatic relations between China and the Vatican – the only European government that still recognises the Republic of China Government on Taiwan.

Beijing has announced that before diplomatic relations can be established, two conditions must be met. First, the Vatican must break relations with Taiwan. Second, the Vatican must agree not to interfere in China's internal affairs 'in the guise of religious affairs'.

The Vatican has made it clear that the first condition is not a problem. After all, the church can function in Taiwan, which allows freedom of religion, even in the absence of diplomatic relations. But the second condition is an issue since the church feels that the appointment of Chinese bishops is a religious affair and not an internal affair of the Chinese state.

A practical problem is the future of the Chinese Patriotic Catholic Association, the government-sponsored body set up in 1957, which does not recognise the supremacy of the Pope.

Since the patriotic association was set up specifically to sever the Chinese church from Rome, it is difficult to see what role it can play if the Chinese Government itself recognises the authority of the Pope over the Church in China.

Moreover, the patriotic association supports government policies that contravene Catholic teachings on such issues as abortion and contraception. Although, in theory, the

Catholic Church in China is divided – with an illegal, underground church that recognises the authority of the Pope and an official, patriotic church that does not – in reality, many priests and bishops who are part of the patriotic association secretly proclaim allegiance to the Pope.

In October 2007, when Pope Benedict XVI convened a synod of bishops, he invited three bishops of the patriotic association as well as an underground bishop to attend. In the end, none of them went to Rome because the Chinese Government did not allow them to travel.

Perhaps the most important obstacle to normalisation is something that Beijing has not articulated in public: a fear that the Catholic Church might subvert the Chinese Communist Party and bring about its downfall. Beijing certainly remembers the role played by Pope John Paul II, who was widely seen as being partly responsible for the fall of the communist regime in Poland in particular and those in Eastern Europe in general.

Ironically, while there were only about a million Christians in China in 1949, there are 70 million to 80 million today as many people who have lost faith in communism have turned elsewhere for spiritual solace.

Islam

Christians are by no means the only ones subject to severe political pressure. According to the US Commission on

International Religious Freedom, a body mandated by Congress to monitor abuse of freedom of religion around the world, religious communities 'that have been targeted in particular include Uighur Muslims, Tibetan Buddhists, "unregistered" Roman Catholics and Protestants, and various spiritual movements such as Falun Gong.'[1]

The majority of Muslims live in north-western China, mainly in the region of Xinjiang but also in Gansu, Ningxia and Qinghai provinces. There is a separatist movement among the Uigurs in Xinjiang, and China has labelled such groups terrorists. Some Uigurs arrested by the United States in Afghanistan had been trained by al-Qaeda. When the US decided they were not a threat, these Uigurs who had been kept in Guantánamo refused to be sent back to China for fear of persecution and the US sent some of them to Albania

Falun Gong

The Falun Gong was officially denounced as an 'evil cult' in 1999 and, since then, its members have endured serious persecution, including torture. Falun Gong is a form of *qigong* whose practitioners do meditation exercises and seek to develop their hearts and characters according to the principles of truthfulness, compassion, and forbearance. It has millions of members. It was targeted by the state after Falun Gong members surrounded Communist Party headquarters in Beijing in 1999 to protest against ill treatment in another city. The Communist Party, realising that here was a huge organisation not under its control, decided to crack down on its members.

According to a US Commission on International Religious Freedom report in May 2006, 'Tens of thousands of Falun Gong practitioners have been sent to labour camps without trial or sent to mental health institutions for re-education due to their affiliation with an "evil cult". Falun Gong practitioners claim that between 1,000 and 2,000 practitioners have been killed as a result of police brutality. Given the lack of judicial transparency, the number and treatment of Falun Gong practitioners in confinement is difficult to confirm.'[2] Nevertheless, the report said,

> . . . there is substantial evidence from foreign
> diplomats, international human rights groups, and
> human rights activists in Hong Kong that the
> crackdowns on the Falun Gong continue to be
> widespread and violent . . . In the past year, a
> growing number of reports have surfaced regarding
> the re-arrest of Falun Gong practitioners who have
> been released after completing terms of
> imprisonment originating from the original
> crackdown in 1999 and 2000. In addition, the
> Chinese Government has reportedly continued to
> pressure foreign businesses in China to sign

statements denouncing the Falun Gong and to refuse to employ the group's followers.

In the end, the tension between the communists and theists is that of opposing ideologies. The Communist Party does not accept the dictum 'Render unto Caesar the things which are Caesar's, and unto God the things that are God's' because communism is not just a form of government but an alternative belief system. The Communist Party wants to play the role of both Caesar and God.

3.

The Health of the Nation

China's treatment of health issues, like much of its conduct since the reform and opening period ushered in by Deng Xiaoping in the late 1970s, was characterised by hesitation and half steps. It did not quite know how to deal with new diseases, especially HIV/AIDs, and for a long time acted as though this was only a foreigners' disease that Chinese people did not have to worry about.

HIV/AIDS

Initially, the government reacted to the appearance of AIDS overseas by barring HIV-infected persons from entering the country. However, in the late 1980s and early 1990s, an AIDS epidemic broke out among drug users in Yunnan province, next to Burma, now Myanmar.

But it was the explosion of HIV cases in Henan province among people who were neither foreigners nor drug users that finally woke China up to the very real threat posed by the disease. In Henan, about a million poor farmers tried to supplement their income by selling their blood on a regular basis. However, those in charge of the blood donation systems ignored the most basic steps to prevent the spread of disease. They reused tubes used to collect blood. Much worse, they pooled red cells from different donors and re-injected the pooled blood into each person.

As a result, up to a million people were infected in the province, which was dubbed by the *Guardian* as the 'ground zero' of 'arguably the world's worst HIV/AIDS epidemic'.

Once HIV was introduced into Henan, it spread quickly and in a number of villages the majority of the population became infected. Soon, HIV cases linked to blood donation were reported from other provinces as well.

SARS

While AIDS was introduced into China from abroad, SARS, or Severe Acute Respiratory Syndrome was a Chinese export.

Until 2003, the rest of the world did not realise that China treated major health issues the way it treated almost everything else: as state secrets. Until then, it probably did not matter much but after the outbreak of SARS the world discovered that its health was at risk because China restricted information about epidemics.

In November 2002, an outbreak of a mysterious kind of 'atypical pneumonia' took place in Guangdong province, adjoining Hong Kong. Chinese government officials were not sure what to make of it and did not inform the World Health Organization of the outbreak until February 2003, restricting media coverage so as not to create a panic. This cover-up of the disease led to it spreading outside rural Guangdong to urban Hong Kong, where it quickly migrated to other countries.

Dr Gao Yaojie, AIDS activist

Into the tragic scene of China's HIV/AIDS epidemic stepped Dr Gao Yaojie, a gynaecologist and academic who became an AIDS activist in Zhengzhou, the capital of Henan province. Dr Gao visited over a hundred villages in Henan to do AIDS prevention work and to treat people afflicted with AIDS at her own expense and to take care of children orphaned by AIDS. She published a book, *Prevention of AIDS and Sexually Transmitted Diseases*, and distributed 300,000 copies of the book. She was a genuine people's hero.

But her work embarrassed the authorities in Henan by exposing how HIV was spread in the province through illegal blood sales. In 2001, she was awarded the Jonathan Mann Award for Global Health and Human Rights, but the local authorities put her under house arrest and she was prevented from receiving the award in person. In 2003, she was honoured with the Ramon Magsaysay Award for public service. Again, she was prevented from going to the Philippines to receive the award.

In 2007, she was chosen by Vital Voices Global Partnership, a non-profit group, to receive its Global Women's Leadership Award for Human Rights. Again, the provincial authorities put the seventy-nine-year-old doctor under house arrest. It was only after Senator Hillary Clinton intervened that Beijing allowed Dr Gao to leave the country to receive the award.

When she was in the United States, she said that the situation in China was improving, since for the first time she was actually allowed to receive an award.

When Hong Kong's director of health, Margaret Chan (now the director general of the WHO), tried to get information from China, she failed because, she was told, infectious diseases were state secrets.

By spring, more than 300 people in Guangdong had been stricken, of whom five had died. But while the disease originated in southern China, it centred on Hong Kong because it was from Hong Kong, an aviation hub, that the disease spread quickly to South East Asia, Europe and Canada.

On 17 March 2003, when at least nine people around the world were known to have died, the WHO issued a worldwide alert. Gro Harlem Bruntlandt, director general of the WHO, called the new syndrome a worldwide health threat.

But even after the WHO alert, Chinese officials did not immediately co-operate, denying permission for WHO experts to travel to Guangdong to study the situation there for a week. Health Minister Zhang Wenkang gave a press conference on 3 April assuring the world that everything was fine, that Beijing had only a handful of SARS cases and inviting foreigners to visit the capital.

But then something unexpected happened. Jiang Yanyong, a renowned surgeon, exposed the real situation by writing a letter to the world media, which was put by *Time* magazine on its website. He contested the official number of SARS cases and said that staff at military hospitals had been ordered to keep the disease a secret. 'As a doctor,' he wrote, 'I have a responsibility to aid international and local efforts to prevent the spread of SARS.'

By then, at least 98 people around the world had died and several thousand had been infected. Canada was especially hard hit, with at least 10 fatalities and more than 180 reported cases.

It had also become clear that the Chinese Government had been less than honest in its dealings with the WHO. Li Liming, director of the Chinese Centre for Disease Control and Prevention, made a public apology in an attempt to control the damage to China's international image. 'Today, we apologise to everyone,' Mr Li said. 'Our medical departments and our mass media suffered poor co-ordination. We weren't able to muster our forces in helping provide everyone with scientific publicity and allowing the masses to get hold of this sort of knowledge.'[1]

But while Mr Li blamed poor co-ordination, the reality was that the media had been forbidden from reporting on the outbreak. Even after the apology, Beijing played down the severity of the outbreak, lying about the actual number of cases. The authorities in Guangdong as well as Health Minister Zhang announced that the disease was under control.

Mr Zhang insisted that even though there were more cases of SARS in China than anywhere else, the disease may not have originated in Guangdong, or even in China.

Part of the problem was that Chinese law forbade the disclosure of certain health information. Outbreaks of such infectious diseases as viral hepatitis and epidemic haem-orrhagic fever are treated as state secrets. This is because traditionally China sought to suppress any information that portrayed the country in a negative light.

In his own defence, Zhang said, 'What we have done is to give timely notice about the pneumonia, in accordance with our national conditions and law.' He did not explain that Chinese law prevented the giving out of timely notice. Meanwhile, the official Chinese media denounced those who were critical of Beijing's handling of the SARS crisis as members of an 'anti-China clique'.

On 18 April, Premier Wen Jiabao, realising the gravity of the situation, reversed the government's position and called for accurate reporting of the SARS crisis. Two days later, Beijing dramatically raised the official count of SARS cases from 37 to 339. Minister Zhang and Beijing Mayor Meng Xuenong, who had participated in the cover-up, were fired. China made an about-turn in its policy. It would co-operate with the WHO and the international community.

A major threshold had been crossed. China had decided to make itself more transparent and accountable so that it would be accepted by the international community and be able to play a bigger role in the world.

China's new approach appeared to have been confirmed at the end of the year when a new case of SARS appeared in Guangzhou and the government notified the WHO six days later. Despite the delay, the world organisation was full of praise for China's co-operative attitude.

However, the WHO was not notified of another case, that of a waitress who fell ill on 25 December, until 8 January. After that, WHO officials made it clear that they would like China to make more information available to them, and much more promptly.

Dr Jiang Yanyong's courage in exposing China's cover-up of the SARS outbreak was recognised internationally. In 2004, the Ramon Magsaysay Award for public service was given to Dr Jiang in recognition of 'his brave stand for truth in China, spurring life-saving measures to confront and contain the deadly threat of SARS.'

However, the Chinese Government refused to allow him to leave the country to receive the award. Presumably, China did not want the world to be reminded of its cover-up, an act that led to the deaths of hundreds of people outside the mainland.

Avian Flu

In 2004, a new threat emerged – the highly pathogenic H5N1 bird flu. The WHO repeatedly called on China to take urgent action against avian flu, warning that the window of opportunity was closing fast. News that the disease had spread to Anhui, Shanghai and Guangdong caused the WHO to declare that this latest news strongly suggested that the window was getting smaller with each passing day.

The WHO called on China to provide samples so that the viruses could be studied, to share more information about the disease, to step up monitoring for possible human cases and to take precautions so that workers engaged in the mass slaughter of birds were not accidentally infected.

But Beijing was again dragging its feet. The Chinese

Ministry of Health did not report on a new case of SARS until after the patient had made a full recovery and was discharged from hospital. The patient, a forty-year-old director of a hospital from Guangzhou who developed SARS symptoms on 7 January, was admitted to hospital on 16 January with pneumonia and was discharged on 30 January. On 31 January, China informed the WHO.

Beijing, it appeared, was still more concerned with saving face than with saving lives. Its co-operation with the WHO still leaves much to be desired. Of course, disclosing the presence of SARS or bird flu might result in a loss of tourists and foreign investment, but potential threats to the health of the international community ought not to be treated by China as state secrets – they are the whole world's affair.

From State Secrets to Global Co-operation

On the whole, however, China is continuing to open up. In 2004, China announced the opening of its diplomatic archives for the first time since the People's Republic was established and, subsequently, there was an announcement that public security bodies, such as the police, were establishing a system to disclose information to the public. The steps taken are small, but at least they are moving in the right direction.

In 2005, the definition of state secrets was changed. From now on, people were told, the number of people killed in natural disasters will no longer be considered a state secret. Increasingly, the government is coming to accept that the public has a right to know.

Still, progress is likely to be slow. Thus, in 2005, an AIDS activist, Wan Yanhai, was arrested for disclosing details about China's HIV problem. Information about infectious diseases, it turned out, still could not be disclosed because they were state secrets. Because of its obsession with state secrets, China hurts not only itself but the rest of the world as well. If reliable information on infectious diseases is not available, then doctors and researchers will not be able to fight them effectively.

After Deng Xiaoping came to power in the late 1970s, he repeatedly called on people to seek truth from facts, to be practical, to recognise reality and to overcome problems. However, if facts are covered up, if they are stamped 'state secrets', then it no longer becomes possible to seek truth from facts, because truth is not available.

In November 2005, China appealed to the WHO for help to determine whether three cases of 'pneumonia caused by unknown factors' in Hunan province could have been the result of the H5N1 virus. This was a significant move since it showed that Beijing was taking the threat of bird flu seriously.

Prior to that, Chinese health authorities had denied that two children in Xiangtan county in Hunan province – a twelve-year-old girl who died and her younger brother, aged nine, both of whom had eaten a sick chicken – had caught the bird flu virus. The third case is a thirty-six-year-old teacher who had handled chickens with a cut on his hand.

However, the Ministry of Health said on 6 November 2005 that 'the possibility of human infection of the highly deadly H5N1 strain of bird flu cannot be ruled out' and called on the WHO to help in testing blood and throat swabs from the three victims.

The move was viewed positively because China had not reported a single case of human infection of the H5N1 virus while scores had been reported in South East Asia.

One problem in China is that farmers frequently cannot afford to kill their poultry even when ordered to do so because the government compensation is seen as inadequate. That is why there have been cases of people who ate dead or sick chickens, not realising the risk that they were taking.

In summer 2006, use of a defective antibiotic led to at least six deaths before the drug was banned. According to the *Beijing News*, the first notice of an adverse reaction to the drug was posted on the State Food and Drug Administration (SFDA) website on 27 July, but the drug was not banned until a week later.

Containing the Spread of Information

Despite the high cost China has paid for its mishandling of HIV/AIDS and SARS, it does not appear to have fundamentally changed its values, aside from being slightly more open and willing to provide information to the WHO.

In spring 2008, the New York-based Asia Catalyst group reported that China was expanding its crackdown on health websites and had shut down two popular websites for people with AIDS and hepatitis and threatened the shutdown of a third unless it removed 'illegal information'. It said China should allow AIDS and hepatitis groups free access to the Internet to fight the epidemics. 'The Internet is a lifeline to thousands of people suffering from AIDS and hepatitis around China,' said Sara Davis, executive director of Asia Catalyst. 'Shutting down websites will only drive those people further underground.'

On 20 November 2007, the Beijing Communications Administration ordered the shutdown of www.hbvhbv.com, a popular forum known as 'In the Hepatitis B Camp Network of China'. Registered users share information, including warnings about the fake hepatitis medicines that proliferate in China. The forum is run by Beijing Yirenping, a health and welfare organisation.

On 26 February 2008, authorities shut down the AIDS Museum site (www.aidsmuseum.net), an AIDS news site, and www.aidswiki.cn, a collaborative 'wiki' through which

AIDS advocates shared news and drafted articles. According to its host, AIDS advocate Chang Kun, the site boasted 300,000 visits per day.

On 5 March, China's leading independent AIDS organisation, Aizhixing, was warned to remove unspecified 'illegal information' from its website, www.aizhi.net, and the site was shut down.

The web crackdown follows on the arrest of AIDS and civil rights advocate Hu Jia, who was detained in December 2007 and was sentenced to three and a half years in prison for 'inciting state subversion'. His wife, Zeng Jinyan, and their baby both remain under house arrest. In a public statement, Aizhixing suggested their website troubles could be linked to reports on their site about Hu Jia.

Widespread stigma and discrimination has driven many people with HIV/AIDS and hepatitis underground in China, making the Internet the only way anonymous users can gain basic information about their health and legal rights. There are an estimated 130 million people carrying the hepatitis B virus in China. Officially China admits to having 650,000 people with HIV/AIDs, though independent experts believe the number may be higher.

China's actions appear to be at odds with its international obligations. The International Covenant on Economic, Social and Cultural Rights, which China has ratified, guarantees everyone the right to health, including the right to access health information. Shutting down websites that provide crucial information to disease sufferers is a violation of their human rights.

Modern technology is making it more difficult for the government to control information. Creeping privatisation through state subcontracting of private media enterprises may continue, and competition between local and national state-owned media organisations could encourage stories on a wider range of topics. The Internet and foreign media organisations are also sources of information. So far the government has been trying to control all such sources of information. It should realise that such efforts are counter-productive.

4.

Working the Media

Article 35 of the Chinese Constitution guarantees freedom of the press along with other rights, but this freedom is hemmed in by laws and regulations that make it virtually meaningless.

For one thing, other provisions of the constitution can be interpreted in such a way as to severely limit press freedom. For example, Article 51 says that citizens, in the exercise of their freedoms and rights, 'may not infringe upon the interests of the state, of society and of the collective or upon the lawful rights and freedoms of other citizens.' Article 53 says it is the duty of all citizens to 'keep state secrets', without defining what they are or how an ordinary person may come into possession of them. And Article 54 says it is the duty of citizens 'to safeguard the security, honour and interests of the motherland', a duty that may conceivably require the suppression of negative information.

Moreover, there are other laws and regulations that specifically curb the right of the media to disseminate information and the right of citizens to receive it. For example, there is the 'Protection of National Secrets Law' promulgated in May 1989 and the June 1992 'Regulation on the Protection of Secrets for News and Publication'.

The former law applies to media reports on military affairs, projects for 'economic and social development', technological development, criminal investigations by national security agencies, or other subjects determined by state institutions to be 'secret' in nature.[1] The regulation echoes such sentiments.

And the 'Rule on Strengthening Management over Publications Concerning Important Party and National Leaders', issued in 1990, makes it illegal to report on any aspect of the lives of top leaders without permission from the Central Propaganda Department and other central government ministries.

In addition to the Propaganda Department, there is another institution called the General Administration for Press and Publications. The general administration in 2007 reminded the press that 'reports must be true, precise, objective, fair and should not oppose the interests of the state or infringe the rights of citizens.'[2]

Among the host of regulations that journalists operate under are the Regulations for the Administration of Publishing. Article 26 says, among other things, that no publication may contain anything that 'jeopardises the unity, sovereignty or territorial integrity of the state' or that 'divulges state secrets, jeopardises national security, or is detrimental to the dignity and interests of the state'.

There are also Regulations for the Administration of Radio and Television which, after listing all the forbidden content, adds: 'other materials which are prohibited by laws and administrative rules and regulations'.

Online publishing is governed by its own set of rules, which are spelled out in Provisional Rules for the Administration of Online Publishing. And then, of course, there are the Provisions on the Administration of Internet News Information Services as well as the Secrecy Rules in Respect of News Publishing.

Article 5 of the Secrecy Rules says, 'News publishing entities and entities supplying information shall establish sound systems for the censorship of secrets in news publishing in accordance with the state laws and regulations regarding secrecy.'

As for how this is to be done, Article 6 advises: 'Systems for the censorship of secrets in news publishing shall implement a combination of self-censorship and external censorship.'

And then there is the dreaded Law of the People's Republic of China on Guarding State Secrets. As we have already seen, according to this law there are many kinds of state secrets, including those concerning major policy decisions on state affairs; on national defence; on diplomatic activities; on economic and social development as well as on science and technology. Of course, there are also 'other matters that are classified as state secrets'.

It is increasingly obvious that China's obsession with secrecy is coming into conflict with international obligations that it assumed by ratifying treaties on human rights, which invariably call for periodic reports to ensure that a signatory state is living up to its commitments.

One example is CEDAW, the Convention on the Elimination of All Forms of Discrimination Against Women. In August 2006, the United Nations committee charged with overseeing the implementation of the convention expressed regret that China's report failed to provide sufficient data, as well as analytical information on the de facto situation of women. The committee also asked for information on Tibet, one of the most politically sensitive regions in the country. It also called on Beijing to adopt laws and regulations relating to the status of refugees and asylum seekers, in particular, North Korean women.

Human Rights in China, a non-governmental organisation based in New York, said in a report that much of the data required by the committee is classified as state secrets in China. This includes statistics on kidnapping and trafficking, induced abortions, infanticide and the gender ratio.

If journalists violate official directives, they may be punished, sometimes physically. On 16 August 2007, the Propaganda Department ordered the Chinese media to restrict coverage of a bridge collapse that killed more than forty people in the city of Fenghuang, in Hunan province. Media were forced to pull out their reporters from the city. Before they could leave, five journalists, including one from *Nanfang Dushi Bao*, were beaten by men linked to the local authorities.[3]

Laws and regulations are often vaguely worded and allow officials to interpret them according to the wishes of party leaders.

Glossary of Censorship

The international journalists association Reporters Without Borders compiled an internal document that detailed different forms of censorship. It reported that the Propaganda Department warned publications in the form of a glossary. 'Reporting banned' means: it is forbidden to write a report on this subject; 'Don't send a reporter' means: permission to publish the standard article from the Xinhua agency or to copy the report or article from local media; 'Ban on criticism' means: no comment on the remarks, including with a cartoon.[4]

Key Players in the Media

Even within the Chinese media, there are gradations of control. The *People's Daily*, the official newspaper of the Chinese Government and the Communist Party, is the country's major mouthpiece. Anything that appears in that newspaper can be considered authoritative. It has no independence to speak of.

Alongside the *People's Daily*, there are other news outlets directly controlled by the state, such as the Xinhua News Agency, China Radio International, China Central Television and *Guangming Daily*, all of which are controlled by party cadres in the government and the Propaganda Department. They are not businesses as such; their goal is not to make money but to disseminate the party line.

'Everyone in the newsroom knows that we have to wait for the story from the official news agency Xinhua when there is an issue relating to party leaders, official appointments or international subjects such as North Korea,' a journalist on the *Beijing News* told Geneva-based Reporters Without Borders. 'It is much too risky to publish anything before then. Everyone knows what is banned: minorities, religious freedom and Falun Gong.'[5]

Xinhua functions as an official news agency and its reports, certainly on events in China, are considered author-itative, the equivalent of government announcements. In addition, though, it also provides confidential information for senior officials. Many reports by Xinhua reporters that are considered unsuitable for general consumption are published for internal consumption only by senior officials.

On the sixtieth anniversary of the establishment of Xinhua, celebrated on 31 May 2007, Liu Yunshan, director of the Propaganda Department, described the agency's role as follows:

> It should forcefully propagandise China's policy and advocacy of adhering to scientific development, harmonious development, and peaceful development; should fully present China's brand new outlook of economic development, social progress, ethnic solidarity, and the people living and working in peace and contentment; should fully reflect the Chinese people's good wish to pursue world harmony and to promote peace of mankind; and should create an image of China as being civilised, just, democratic, and progressive.

Aside from central-level organisations, there are also provincial and municipal media outlets, controlled by local governments at that level. But even though those media are primarily propaganda organs, many of them also have commercial spin-offs, such as the Nanfang Daily Group in Guangdong province, whose operations are clearly for profit.

In addition, there are also purely commercial news media. The best example of this is *Caijing*, a financial magazine based in Beijing, which has a solid reputation for well-researched journalism. Its reports on SARS, avian influenza, pharmaceutical scams, corruption, and other crucial issues have won it an affluent readership and wide admiration.

Interestingly enough, publishing and broadcasting have been growth industries in China, even though the state has shut down hundreds of television stations and newspapers for publishing internal news. Since 1979, when the sale of advertisements in state-controlled newspapers became legal, the media industry has undergone a dramatic commercial reform. In 2006, advertising revenue in China shot up 22 per cent, to 386.6 billion yuan ($51 billion), as income from newspaper and especially television and magazine advertising grew dramatically, according to figures from Nielsen Media Research.[6]

Publications that focus on non-political topics, such as sports, culture, fashion or economics, have greater leeway because what they write about is not politically sensitive. *Caijing* magazine has also avoided being influenced by advertisers by having a firewall between the editorial and business teams.

The magazine is owned by the SEEC Media Group and comes under the umbrella of the All-China Federation of

Industry and Commerce, an official organisation that is viewed as being more open and liberal. However, even *Caijing* can get into trouble. For example, in March 2007 when the magazine was planning to publish an article about controversial legislation to protect private property, the issue was pulled at the last minute. The article was revised and appeared in the magazine's next issue.

A crusading editor can get into trouble even when his crusade is successful. In 2004, a college graduate, Sun Zhigang, was taken into police custody and beaten to death simply because he was not carrying proper identity documentation. Powerful reporting by the newspaper *Nanfang Dushi Bao* forced the government to change nationwide detention policies. However, its editor, Cheng Yizhong, was held in police custody for five months and two of his colleagues were sent to prison ostensibly on corruption charges.

Freedom of the Press

To ensure control of the media, China does not permit foreigners to invest in the Chinese media. In fact, the State Council has issued a directive that non-public capital cannot set up and operate a news agency, a newspaper, a publishing house, a radio station, or a TV station. In addition, radio and TV signal broadcasting and relay stations, satellites and backbone networks are closed to non-public capital.[7]

In its report on China in 2007, Amnesty International said: 'The government's crackdown on journalists, writers, and Internet users intensified. Numerous popular newspapers and journals were shut down. Hundreds of international websites remained blocked and thousands of Chinese websites were shut down. Dozens of journalists were detained for reporting on sensitive issues.'

Meanwhile, the international journalists association Reporters Without Borders in 2007 ranked China among the worst countries in the world in terms of press freedom, at 163 among 169 countries and in the company of such countries as Burma, North Korea and Eritrea. It said:

> With its position in the ranking unchanged since last year, China continues to pursue very repressive policies towards the Internet. Five major censorship bodies, including those operated directly by the government and the Communist Party's publicity department (the former propaganda department), control the flow of news and information online.

> Censorship ranges from imprisoning online journalists to replacing taboo words such as '4 June', 'Tiananmen' and 'conservative wing of the Communist Party of China' with asterisks. Censorship may be applied both before and after publication of a news report.[8]

The Communist Party maintains control of the news media primarily through its Propaganda Department (now renamed the Publicity Department in English though the Chinese name is unchanged). The Propaganda Department is extremely hands-on in its control of the media.

For example, Reporters Without Borders reported that in November 2007,

> The Propaganda Department ordered the managers of China's leading media to avoid negative reports on air pollution, relations with Taiwan or the question of the Olympic torch and public health problems linked to the preparation of the Olympic Games. Censorship was even tougher for TV and radio with journalists working for state-run CCTV receiving a daily warning when they switch on their work computers about subjects to avoid or those to handle with caution. For example, in December they were banned from covering the case of the death in hospital of a pregnant woman for lack of medical attention. They were also ordered to restrict comment on the assassination of Pakistani opposition leader Benazir Bhutto, so as to avoid offending China's ally Pakistan.[9]

Freezing Point

One example of how propaganda officials handle journalists who depart from the party line is the case of the publication *Bing Dian*, or *Freezing Point*, the weekly supplement of the state-run *China Youth Daily*, in 2006. The four-page supplement was shut down because of an article that it ran about events that took place a century ago.[10]

The article, written by a scholar Yuan Weishi of Zhongshan University in Guangzhou, was critical of the official depiction of China's relations with the West in the late nineteenth century. Yuan took issue with a history textbook used in China's secondary schools. One focus of his criticism was the depiction of the Boxer Uprising of 1900. (The Boxer Rebellion was an uprising against foreign influence in areas such as trade, politics, religion and technology. Its members were called Boxers by Westerners because of the martial arts they practised.) In one month, Professor Yuan wrote, 231 foreigners were killed, including 53 children. As for Chinese victims, Yuan wrote that in Shanxi province alone, more than 5,700 Catholics were killed and, in Liaoning province, more than 1,000 followers were killed.

Commenting on the use of history to instil nationalistic feelings, Yuan wrote: 'It is obvious that we must love our country. But there are two ways to love our country.' 'The traditional approach,' he said, 'was to inflame nationalistic passions – in the selection and presentation of historical materials, [to use only] those that favour China whether they are true or false.' He called for a more balanced approach in which events are analysed rationally. 'If it is right, it is right and if it is wrong, it is wrong,' he said. But his approach did not find favour with China's censors.

The decision to shut down *Freezing Point* was disclosed by the Propaganda Department to media around the country. They were instructed to 'not report or comment on the stoppage of *Freezing Point*', and 'not attend any press conference given by the editorial and reporting staff of *Freezing Point*'. The supplement's editor, Li Datong, learned about the closure of his publication from friends in the media who had received the Propaganda Department's instructions. He himself was the last to be officially informed.[11]

Li Datong was a veteran journalist and party member. Actually, he was in the news even before the Yuan Weishi incident. The previous summer, he openly attacked a plan by the newspaper to alter the pay structure by awarding bonuses to reporters on the basis of who won praise from government officials. Those criticised by officials would have pay deducted.

Li Datong wrote a letter to the newspaper's editor-in-chief, Li Erliang, which was subsequently leaked. In the letter, he said of the plan:

This means that no matter how much effort was put into your report, no matter how difficult your investigation was, no matter how well written your report was, and even if your life had been threatened during the process (and enough reporters have been beaten up for trying to report the truth), and no matter how much the readers praised the report, as long as some official is unhappy and makes a few 'critical' comments, then all your work is worth zero, you have added zero to the reputation of the newspaper and your readers' opinions are worth less than a fart – in fact, you will be penalised as much as this month's wages!

As a result, the newspaper scrapped the proposed bonus plan.

Journalists Who Speak Out

Sometimes journalists who take their jobs too seriously are simply removed and assigned to innocuous publications. For example, Huang Liangtian, editor of the monthly *Bai Xing* (*The Masses*) in 2007, was transferred to a small agricultural magazine after he investigated harsh conditions in rural areas. He had also revealed that the administration of a poor region in Henan province had built a square larger than

Tiananmen in Beijing.

'I doubt that freedom of the press will improve for government media and I am sad that my life as a journalist stops here,' Huang Liangtian told Reporters Without Borders.[12]

China frequently accuses journalists and others of leaking state secrets, a charge that automatically results in closed hearings in court. There are more journalists, cyber-dissidents, Internet-users and freedom of expression campaigners jailed in China than in any other country.[13]

'They frequently endure harsh prison conditions,' the journalists association reported. 'They share overcrowded cells with criminals, are condemned to forced labour and are regularly beaten by their guards or by fellow prisoners. Ill-treatment is at its worst in the first weeks in custody when police try to extract confessions. At least 33 journalists were in prison in China as at 1st January 2008.'

The World Wide Web

The rise of the Internet has created new opportunities and challenges for China's censors. There is now talk of tens of thousands of web policemen who patrol the Internet. According to Reporters Without Borders, since August 2007, two cyber-police have been regularly popping up on the screens of computers in Internet cafés to remind users that they are being monitored. Fifty cyber-dissidents are currently detained in China because of their online activities.[14]

Whenever a big story breaks, the censors swing into action. So when reports emerged that hundreds, perhaps thousands – the majority of them children – were being forced to work as slaves in brick kilns in Shanxi and Henan provinces, the party, through the Internet Bureau of its Central Office of External Communication, issued a directive on 15 June 2007 that said:

> Regarding the Shanxi 'illegal brick kilns' event, all websites should reinforce positive propaganda, put more emphasis on the forceful measures that the central and local governments have already taken, and close the comment function in the related news reports. The management of the interactive communication tools, such as online forums, blogs and instant messages, should also be strengthened. Harmful information that uses this event to attack the party and government should be deleted as soon as possible. All local external communication offices should enhance their instruction, supervision and inspection and concretely implement the related management measures.[15]

In late 2005, the government shut down a popular Chinese-language blog maintained by journalist Zhao Jing, a research assistant for the *New York Times* who used the pen name Michael Anti. The site had been critical of the firing of top editors at the *Beijing News*, a newspaper known for its aggressive reporting.

The dismissal prompted a hundred journalists at the paper to go on strike, calling for the reinstatement of its editor, Yang Bin. Yang and two of his deputies were suddenly removed after the paper published stories on the cover-up of a massive benzene chemical spill in the Songhua river.

In its web-linked censorship efforts, China has enlisted the assistance of foreign corporations. Thus, at Beijing's request, Microsoft's weblog service censors terms such as democracy and human rights.

In 2005, Yahoo was the target of sharp criticism after it acknowledged providing information that was used against reporter Shi Tao of *Contemporary Business News,* in Hunan province. Shi was accused of divulging state secrets abroad. At the request of Chinese security authorities, Yahoo provided information on Shi Tao's Internet protocol (IP) address that made it easy for the police to track him down. He was sentenced to ten years in prison.

His offence? He had released the contents of a government directive, issued as the fifteenth anniversary of the 4 June crackdown in Tiananmen Square drew near. The authorities were fearful that pro-democracy dissidents might return to China to stage demonstrations and so issued 'A notice concerning the work for maintaining stability', which warned the media not to report anything regarding 'the so-called "June 4th event".'

In 2005, Beijing issued rules prohibiting bloggers and other online publishers from posting anything that goes against state security and the public interest. In December 2005, Beijing also announced a new policy under which all mobile-phone subscribers will have to register using their real names. Those who buy prepaid phone cards will have to provide proof of identity.

Relations with Foreign Correspondents

Foreign journalists are less under the control of the Chinese authorities. In fact, new regulations brought in on 1 January 2007 allowed greater freedom of movement for foreign correspondents. They no longer needed official permission to conduct interviews. Some media immediately took advantage of the change to report on subjects that were previously banned. Reuters went to Inner Mongolia to meet the wife of Hada, a local managing editor who has been imprisoned since 1995, an interview which the British agency had been trying to do since 2004. Reuters was also able to interview Bao Tong, former assistant to reformist Prime Minister Zhao Ziyang.

However, despite the new regulations, foreign correspondents were prevented from visiting Zhao Ziyang's children or interviewing Shanghai lawyer Zheng Enchong, lawyer Gao Zhisheng, or AIDS activist Dr Gao Yaojie.[16]

In a press release on 1 January 2008, the Foreign Correspondents Club of China said it had received more than 180 reports of foreign journalists being obstructed in their work since the new rules were introduced. The incidents included threats, physical violence, harassment, the seizure of notes and images, interrogation and visa refusals. In one case, Reuters correspondent Chris Buckley was attacked by ten thugs while reporting on a prison. His equipment was stolen and he was threatened with death.

In another case, Brice Pedroletti, a journalist with the French daily *Le Monde*, was observed while researching a story in Xinjiang. He and the people he interviewed were later followed and interrogated by police.

Cai Wu, the State Council's Information Minister, said in December 2007 that China would have a wider attitude toward the world and ensure better services for the media in the future. He said his office was helping to train local officials to do this. The training, he said, was aimed at changing the mentality of news officials and government leaders at different levels and preparing them to face the outside world more openly.

Foreigners in China have access to media outlets not available to most Chinese. However, even those are subject to censorship. In March 2008, when violent demonstrations broke out in Tibet, CNN and BBC television were briefly blacked out whenever reports turned to Tibet. The screen would suddenly go black and stay that away until the news announcer turned to another topic.

The Challenges of Technology

China has traditionally used its control of information to keep its people in check. However, the advance of technology is making this more difficult. True, the government is attempting to keep up with the times with the introduction of cyber-policemen, but it is a losing battle.

In this age of instant messaging, the government is going to find it increasingly difficult to manipulate the news to keep people ignorant, especially when so many of them are now travelling abroad. The government would be better off allowing a free press while retaining official mouthpieces so that its side of the story will always be told.

5.

Economy and Environment

Thirty years ago, China was one of the poorest countries on earth. But in the last twenty-five years it has been the fastest growing major nation with an average annual GDP growth rate above 10 per cent. Today, China possesses the world's fourth largest economy – behind the United States, Japan and Germany – and is an engine of growth for the rest of the world. Its GDP grew 10.7 per cent in 2007 and is expected to grow by an additional 8.7 per cent in 2008.

However, although the size of the Chinese economy is huge, and in all likelihood will become the world's largest in a matter of decades, in per capita terms the country is still poor, being ranked at only 104th in the world, according to the International Monetary Fund.

Moreover, the country has paid a huge price for its

rapid growth. China is the world's second largest greenhouse gas emitter behind the United States, and may well by now be number one. And, according to the World Bank, sixteen of the world's twenty most polluted cities are in China.

Migrant Workers

While the Chinese Government deserves credit for lifting hundreds of millions of people above the poverty line, it still faces major economic development challenges, including the need to create tens of millions of jobs every year to accommodate workers laid off by state-owned enterprises and those entering the job market. While several hundred million people living in major cities along the coast enjoy developed-country lifestyles, China as a whole is still a developing country, with the vast majority of its population living in the countryside.

However, countless millions of rural people are being attracted to the big cities, often to work in atrocious conditions. In a report, New York-based Human Rights Watch said in March 2008 that construction workers in Beijing work in dangerous conditions, have no access to medical treatment, and often go unpaid.[1]

'Despite years of government rhetoric, employers still cheat migrant construction workers of hard-earned wages,' said Sophie Richardson, the group's Asia advocacy director. 'And when it comes to basic social services, the government still discriminates against migrants.'

Millions of other migrant workers toil away in factories in southern China, making toys, furniture, garments and just about anything else that the rest of the world will import. Many of these factories are in Guangdong province, adjoining Hong Kong. Their workers do not have job security, health insurance or pension benefits and are often paid less than their due by their employer. After an incapacitating industrial accident, the worker is simply laid off, with no compensation.

Little wonder, then, that Han Dongfang, a labour activist who heads Hong Kong-based *China Labour Bulletin*, has reported that there is at least one strike every day involving more than a thousand workers in the Pearl river delta area, China's manufacturing hub.[2] Han cited a statistic that workers break or lose 40,000 fingers a year.[3]

One problem is that the Chinese Government does not allow independent labour unions. The only union allowed is the communist-dominated All-China Federation of Trade Unions, which reflects the interests not of the workers but of the party. When the party wants to attract foreign investment into the country, the rights of the workers come a poor second.

At the Coal Face

It is often said that in Asia, life is cheap and this observation is certainly borne out by the situation in China's coal mines. Economic growth requires fuel and, in China, coal

Cheap Goods at a Price

The reason manufacturing facilities have now been relocated to China from many other countries is that costs are much lower, both in terms of land and labour. And to keep costs low, manufacturers cut corners. That is the main reason for the melamine-tainted pet-food scare, toxic cough syrup and toothpaste, fake milk powder and lead paint on toys and countless other unsafe products from China in 2007.

The melamine, it turns out, was added to pet food to make it appear as though it was rich in protein, when it really wasn't. In fact, it turned out that the melamine resulted in the kidneys of cats and dogs being clogged with crystals, killing them.

As for the toxic toothpaste, the manufacturers substituted diethylene glycol for more expensive glycerin, a safe additive used as a thickening agent. However, diethylene glycol, while also sweet and syrupy, is poisonous.

In the end, the international indignation created by reports of unsafe food and drugs may turn out to be the best thing to happen to China, allowing it to create and strengthen regulatory institutions. The country appears to be taking advantage of the global outcry to put its house in order. And to prove to the world that it was serious, China put the former head of the State Food and Drug Administration, Zheng Xiaoyu, on trial and charged him with accepting bribes to approve untested medicine. Zheng was found guilty and executed.

provides 70 per cent of energy needs. Coal mining is the industry with the worst health and safety record in China.

For example, in October 2004, a gas explosion in the Daping mine near the city of Zhengzhou, in Henan province, left 148 dead. The following month, 166 were killed in a coal-mine blast in northern Shaanxi province.

So poor is the country's record that, while the country produced about a third of the world's coal, it accounted for 80 per cent of mining deaths. From 1992 to 2002, 434 miners died in accidents in the United States, 1,020 in India and 59,543 in China. This means that every 1 million tons of coal produced in China cost the lives of almost five men.

The Chinese Government has been deeply embarrassed by mining accidents and has taken steps to close down unsafe mines. In fact, thousands of such mines were closed and mining fatalities dropped to about 3,800 in 2007 – still the highest in the world. Coal prices also rose. One result was that when southern China was struck by the worst sleet and snowstorms in half a century in 2008, there was a shortage of coal, which was needed to fuel its power plants.

Another problem is that while the government allows coal prices to rise and fall, it fixes electricity prices for political reasons, making it impossible for power plants to pass on price increases to their customers. As a result, coal stockpiles dropped as managers of power plants waited for warmer weather, when coal prices would fall.

So when the sudden cold spell came, the country was unprepared. When the coal shortage led to power cuts, miners were told to work through the Chinese New Year holidays to ensure adequate supplies. President Hu Jintao personally inspected a coal mine in Shanxi province and encouraged miners to increase coal supplies in the battle against the cold weather.

Despite improvements in safety, mining accidents continue to occur. In August 2007, 172 miners were killed in Shandong province in eastern China when a nearby river burst its dams and flooded the mine. And, in December, a gas blast at a coal mine in northern China killed 70 miners and trapped 26 underground.

According to Geoffrey Crothall, an editor at *China Labour Bulletin* in Hong Kong, 'Coal mine owners will push their workers harder and harder to extract more coal and make more money, and unfortunately safety just gets left behind.'[4]

China's demand for coal is inexorable. The nation will rely on coal for at least half of its energy needs for the next thirty to fifty years. To make things worse, very often local officials responsible for enforcing safety regulations are also the ones responsible for maximising profits. Often, Beijing's writ does not extend to the localities. As Crothall said, 'The Central government has passed a legislation to shut down illegal mines but the local authorities don't want to let go of the economic incentives they offer. Owners of illegal mines make hefty profits and bribe local authorities.'[5]

Cleaning Up in Harbin

Industrial accidents in China not only lead to immediate deaths: they also lead to the poisoning of the environment, which in many cases means that signs of illness may not appear for years but, in the long run, will cost the lives of huge numbers of people.

One example of such an accident was the explosion at the Jilin Petrochemical Company in November 2005, which killed five workers and injured seventy others. But the long-term costs may well be much greater. The explosion resulted in 100 tons of benzene and other toxic chemicals being thrown into the Songhua river, an important water source in north-eastern China. The Jilin company, a subsidiary of China National Petroleum Corporation, lied and said the explosion caused no pollution. The Jilin provincial government also covered up the accident and did not notify authorities in neighbouring Heilongjiang province for five days that the toxic chemicals were headed their way.

After Heilongjiang was informed, the city government of Harbin, the provincial capital, shut down the water supply. However, it lied about the reason, saying that it was for routine maintenance of the pipes. Eventually, the governor of

Heilongjiang, Zhang Zuoji, said the city had lied because it did not have permission from higher authorities to disclose the spill. China's state secrets laws, it seems, force officials to lie because they need permission to tell the truth.

In the meantime, thousands of people living between Jilin and Harbin were not informed of the spill and apparently drank and used the contaminated water. Benzene poisoning can cause anaemia, cancer and kidney and liver damage.

In this globalised world, covering up the truth can hurt not just one's own citizens but people in other countries as well. SARS was a case in point. And, where the petro-chemical spill was concerned, the polluted waters in the Songhua river flow into the Amur river in Russia.

China's foreign minister, Li Zhaoxing, informed the Russian ambassador of the accident almost two weeks after it occurred, when the hundred tons of benzene were headed for the Russian town of Khabarovsk. He apologised for any harm that might be caused by the 'major environmental pollution incident' to Russian people downstream. The ambassador told him that the response would have been more efficient if China had informed Russia about it sooner. In the end, the damage in Russia appears to have been contained.

Accidents and natural disasters claim over a million casualties a year in China. According to Wang Jikun, a senior official of the Ministry of Public Security, 1.75 million people were injured and 210,000 killed in 2004, with economic losses amounting to US$80.15 billion, or 6 per cent of GDP.

The 'One Child' Policy

Three decades ago, when China decided to focus its energies on economic development rather than political campaigns, it saw its huge population as a major problem and took steps to limit the growth of that problem. The outcome: the 'one child' policy.

As a result, China's demographers estimate that the population now has 300 million to 400 million fewer people. But there are other, much more negative, consequences.

One grave problem is that there is now a severe gender imbalance. Sons have traditionally been prized in China because they can help to farm the land, take care of the parents when they grow old and continue the family line. A girl, however, marries out and becomes part of someone else's family, responsible for taking care of the husband's ageing parents rather than her own.

Added to this, the development of ultrasound technology has resulted in the aborting of millions of female foetuses. Even infanticide occurs, with girls drowned after childbirth or left to die as couples ensure that the one child they are allowed to have will be male.

As a result, China's sex ratio is severely distorted. While births in industrialised countries stand at 103 to 107 boys per 100 girls, in China in 2007 it reached 120.2 boys to 100 girls. This means that by 2020, 40 million Chinese men will not be able to find wives, leading to social instability, increased trafficking in women and other grave social problems. That is to say, it will lead to serious lack of social harmony, the exact opposite of what the government hopes to achieve. (It is illegal to use ultrasound to determine the sex of the foetus and then abort it if it is found to be female.)

Another consequence is that China is now one of the most rapidly ageing countries in the world. It is estimated that if current trends continue, by 2030, one in five people in the country will be over sixty-five years of age, roughly double the current ratio, making developing China's ageing problem as severe as that of industrialised Japan.

Global Warming and Climate Change

China and the United States, the two biggest emitters of carbon in the world, are taking very different approaches in the international discussions on a new treaty to limit greenhouse gases. In December 2007, 187 countries met in Bali and agreed to set 2009 as a deadline for such a treaty. Both China and the United States attended but were opposed to binding commitments on emission reductions.

China's position was presented by Foreign Minister Yang Jiechi at the annual session of the National People's Congress, or parliament. 'Climate change is mainly attributable to long-term emissions by developed countries in the past and their current high per capita levels of emissions,' Yang said. 'The emissions of three Chinese are less than that of one person in developed countries. That is like one person who eats three slices of bread for breakfast, and three people, each of them eats one slice. Who should be on a diet?'[6]

While China thinks the developed countries, which after all were responsible for building up the amount of greenhouse gases in the atmosphere, should take the lead in cutting back, the United States is taking a different position, arguing that it should not have to cut greenhouse gas emissions unless other large emitters, such as China and India, also agree to do so.

Historically, China has contributed less than 8 per cent of the total emissions of carbon dioxide from energy use since 1850, while the United States is responsible for 29 per cent and Western Europe 27 per cent, according to United Nations data. Since there is no doubt that the developed countries are the ones that pumped out the greenhouse gases that are causing global warming now, China understandably feels that it is only right that they should be the ones to spearhead any move to clean up the environment.

The 1997 Kyoto Protocol committed thirty-seven industrialised countries to cut greenhouse gases by an average of 5 per cent between 2008 and 2012. The United States has refused to be bound by its terms. Efforts now are to negotiate a successor to Kyoto that will take effect in 2012.

It may well be true that cuts by developed countries alone will not solve the problem. But developed countries must take the lead and help developing countries reduce emissions by offering them new technology and financial aid. Norway took the lead by committing itself to spend US$500 million a year toward protecting forests in developing countries.

Former US Vice President Al Gore, who won a Nobel Peace Prize for his work on climate change, said in Bali: 'My country's been responsible for obstructing progress here in Bali; we know that. Over the next two years, the United States is going to be somewhere where it is not now. You must anticipate that.'

Much therefore depends on the next American president. It is conceivable that when the United States agrees to accept emission caps, China may be willing to consider them also, but certainly not of the same magnitude. So the principle of common but differentiated responsibilities is vital.

China is now aware that it cannot focus blindly on GDP growth because it is paying a huge environmental price for its development, with severe pollution of virtually all of its lakes and rivers. Beijing has voluntarily taken such steps as seeking to raise energy efficiency and supporting renewable energy resources. It has set energy-efficiency goals but has fallen far short of its own targets.

Conclusion

Many of China's human rights problems can be ameliorated if the government allows a free press, as guaranteed in the Chinese constitution. A free press will be the government's partner in ferreting out wrongdoing around the country, by officials, by entrepreneurs and, yes, by journalists too if they publish fraudulent reports.

The government, of course, has every right to keep its official mouthpieces, and they have their role to play, dispensing the official line on issues. But the country as a whole would benefit if the press was unleashed.

Beijing has promised to improve the lot of foreign correspondents in China. That is welcome but it is even more important to ensure that Chinese reporters also have the freedom to report the news and not simply government information.

A free press will improve government accountability. It will help to create a system of checks and balances. And it will be a major force in the campaign to stamp out corruption in the country – something the Communist Party has failed to do. It will also speed up information on the outbreak of infectious diseases and environmental disasters.

Corruption will be a focus of journalists. Abuses of power by officials will be exposed, including matters such as police torture, not only of dissidents and devotees of Falun Gong and other banned religions but also of run-of-the-mill criminals.

Entrepreneurs who cut corners and produce unsafe toys, food and drugs will also be in the spotlight. Independent journalists can help China gain a new reputation as a producer of safe, inexpensive high-quality products.

The government will, on occasion, be embarrassed by reports in the press, but that is nothing to fear as it happens in every country where the press is free. The government must stop looking at the press as simply a propaganda tool to improve the government's image. A controlled press is not respected by its readers and so its influence is much less than a free, responsible press.

If a free press is to function properly, the Chinese Government must overhaul its laws and regulations regarding state secrets. Every country must have laws to guard state secrets, but if everything is secret, then nothing is secret and the law becomes meaningless. Recent moves to relax the rules of secrecy are a step in the right direction. Such 'secrets' can potentially do a lot of harm, as was the case when information about the SARS virus was suppressed.

In April 2007, the government adopted nationwide information regulations, accepting the need for the government to be transparent and the right of the public to access information. The regulations, effective from 1 May 2008, were promulgated by the State Council and bind both the central and lower levels of government. But they also emphasised the need to protect secrets and it is still unclear to what extent this will result in government transparency.

Providing information is a big step towards an accountable government. Significantly, the rules require administrations at county level to make public sensitive information on land acquisitions, while village authorities must reveal information on land use and financial accounting.

Disputes over such issues have erupted into violent protests in recent years. Thus, the regulations represent a government attempt to head off future large-scale protests stemming from the actions of local authorities, who provide little compensation to farmers when their land is sold to property developers.

However, the rules also limit the amount of information disclosed, by citing the nebulous concept of state secrets, and exclude information that could threaten national security, public order, economic security and social stability. But it is likely that as people demand more information, the government will have to define the concept of 'state secrets' more precisely.

Even if they do not result in a fully fledged freedom of information system, the rules represent a government attempting to empower the public, or to appear so, and recognise that the government's legitimacy rests on public support.

The Chinese government is already trying to balance economic growth with environmental safety. It needs to do more, in particular by sending the message to officials in the provinces that GDP growth is meaningless if the environment is damaged by poisoning the air and water and by endangering the health of the people.

China should jettison the secretive ways of the past. Stop lying. And, most important of all, the government should accord the highest priority to the health and welfare of the 1.3 billion Chinese people. That should take precedence over economic growth.

The government of President Hu Jintao has repeatedly described itself as a 'people-centred government'. But China still lacks proper legislation to protect personal information. Privacy is a relatively recent concept in China as the government had traditionally meddled in the personal affairs of individuals. Things have improved but there is a need for a privacy law to protect personal information.

At his 2007 annual press conference, Premier Wen Jiabao said that all power is given by the people. Everything belongs to the people, he said, everything should be for the people, everything must rely on people and everything is owed to the people. He also said something reminiscent of remarks made by the late Deng Xiaoping. Deng transformed the concept of socialism by saying that socialist countries could adopt a market economy. A planned economy, he said, is not the definition of socialism because there is planning under capitalism, and the market economy can also function in a socialist country.

Similarly, Mr Wen said that democracy, a legal system, freedom, human rights, equality and fraternity were not peculiar to capitalism. Rather, they are the common achievements of human civilisation made in the long course of history and the common values pursued by the whole of mankind.

China should understand that an open government, accountable to the public, together with elections and an independent judiciary, are essentials in a democracy. Democracy should not be understood as simply the holding of elections. But without elections, there cannot be true democracy.

A more difficult issue is the role of the Communist Party, which currently is above the law. If China is to become a responsible member of the international community, it must adopt a true rule of law, where the judiciary is not subject to the whims of the Party. The Party cannot remain above the law. And if China is to develop a genuine rule of law, what is needed besides independent judges are independent lawyers.

But there have been positive developments. Regulations

issued by China in 2007 to curb the illegal trade in human organs are welcome, especially since they come in the wake of widespread allegations, especially by members of the Falun Gong movement, of such activities. The regulations did not directly address the issue of harvesting organs from executed prisoners but did say that medical personnel and institutions caught illegally harvesting organs for transplant purposes would have their licences suspended or revoked.

Another move to make China a more normal country was a landmark property law in 2007 that grants equal protection to public and private property – a revolutionary move for a country that still calls itself socialist and is run by the Communist Party. The law should go some way towards protecting farmers from illegal land seizures by local officials who make lucrative deals with developers and seize agricultural land for the construction of luxury housing or shopping malls.

Part of the solution to China's human rights problems lies in political reform. Political reform is not a panacea but it does not have to be put off until China becomes a developed country. In fact, it can help China become a developed country.

Reforms relating to press freedom and the judiciary as well as a more open government will vastly improve the human rights situation, even in the absence of an elected government.

With China now a major regional if not yet a global power, it has to act like a responsible power and be willing to be held accountable both to its own people and to the international community.

Public expectations in China have changed tremendously. While in the late 1970s and early 1980s people lived in fear of the government because every act was viewed through a political lens and Mao Zedong's every word was sacred, today no one worships the country's leader as a god. Instead, members of the public know what their rights are and expect the government to honour them.

Perhaps the communists did not mean for people to lose their fear of the party. But clearly, during the last thirty years, there has been a fundamental change in the country. With economic development came not just better food and better clothes, but a new sense of confidence as well. It has given the people the willingness and courage to challenge the government where individuals feel strongly that they are right and that the government is wrong.

The Party deserves credit for the more relaxed political environment of today. The people now live and act with a dignity that they did not know only a decade or two ago. That is something to celebrate and a step forward in the move towards greater human rights.

But a genuine people's republic should be one where the people fully participate in their own governance and are able to make informed choices, including whether they want to keep the ruling party in power. Only if the public has a right to information can its members supervise the operations of the government. And only when the public is in a position to supervise the government can the country properly be called a 'people's republic'.

Notes and References

Introduction

1. Victor Mallet, *Financial Times*, 27 December 2007.

2. Address by State Councillor Tang Jiaxuan, 19 February 2008.

3. Ratification in practice means that the state is bound to abide by the terms of the treaty. Signature alone does not bind the state. It should, however, be noted that China attempts to treat its international obligations seriously.

4. In September 2006, UNESCO Institute for Statistics said that there were 87 million illiterates in China.

Chapter 1: Law and Order

1. Human Rights Report China (includes Tibet, Hong Kong, and Macau). http://guangzhou.usembassy-china.org.cn/hr_report_2007.htm.

2. A court of appeal overturned the conviction, citing insufficient evidence. But after a second trial, Mr Chen was convicted on identical charges and given an identical sentence.

3. See 'State Secrets: China's Legal Labyrinth', Human Rights in China. http://hrichina.org/public/PDFs/State-

Secrets-Report/HRIC_StateSecrets-Report.pdf

4. 'Amendments to Law on Lawyers is a Big Legal
   Move', *China Daily*, 30 October 2007
   http://209.85.175.104/search?q=cache:C2rgn6DQhE
   sJ:news.xinhuanet.com/english/200710/30/content_6
   974179.htm+%22Once+a+person+was+arrested,+he
   +or+she+would+generally+be+considered+a+criminal
   +even+before+being+convicted%22&hl=en&ct=clnk&
   cd=2&gl=hk

5. Memo circulated to author by Nicholas Bequelin.

Chapter 2: A Question of Faith
1. China: USCIRF Calls on President Bush to Request
   Meeting with Prisoners During Beijing Olympics,
   Attend House Church Service.
   http://www.uscirf.gov/mediaroom/press/2008/februar
   y/022808_china.html

2. Annual Report of the United States Commission on
   International Religious Freedom, 2006.
   http://hongkong.usconsulate.gov/uscn_hr_20060503
   01.html

Chapter 3: The Health of the Nation
1. John Pomfret, *Washington Post*, 5 April 2003.

Chapter 4: Working the Media
1. 'Speak No Evil: Mass Media Control in Contemporary
   China', *A Freedom House Special Report*, Ashley
   Esarey, February 2006.

2. Reporters Without Borders, Annual Report 2008: China.
   http://www.rsf.org/article.php3?id_article=25650

3. ibid.

4. ibid.

5. Reporters Without Borders, Annual Report 2008: China.
   http://www.rsf.org/article.php3?id_article=25650

6. Committee to Protect Journalists, *Censorship at Work: The Newsroom in China*.
   http://www.cpj.org/Briefings/2007/Falling_Short/China/5.html

7. China: Clarification of Media Investment Regulations, 18 August 2005.
   http://www.magazine.org/international/13175.cfm

8. 'Eritrea ranked last for first time while G8 members, except Russia, recover lost ground' 16 October 2007.
   http://209.85.175.104/search?q=cache:ExUCanlaCQEJ:www.rsf.org/article.php3%3Fid_article%3D24039+%22press+freedom%22+china+rank+2008&hl=en&ct=clnk&cd=3&gl=hk

9. Reporters Without Borders, Annual Report 2008.

10. 'Leading Publication Shut Down in China', *Washington Post*, 25 January 2006.

11. 'A public protest against the illegal stoppage of the *Freezing Point* weekly magazine', Li Datong,
    http://zonaeuropa.com/20060126_3.htm

12. Reporters Without Borders, Annual Report 2008: China.
    http://www.rsf.org/article.php3?id_article=25650

13. Reporters Without Borders, Annual Report 2008: China.
    http://www.rsf.org/article.php3?id_article=25650

14. 'Eritrea ranked last for first time while G8 members, except Russia, recover lost ground', 16 October 2007. http://209.85.175.104/search?q=cache:ExUCanIaCQE J:www.rsf.org/article.php3%3Fid_article%3D24039+% 22press+freedom%22+china+rank+2008&hl=en&ct=cl nk&cd=3&gl=hk

15. China Digital Times: A Notice from the Central Government to Censor News Related to Shanxi Brick Kilns Event. http://chinadigitaltimes.net/2007/06/a- notice-from-the-central-government-to-censor-news- related-to-shanxi-brick-kilns-event/

16. Reporters Without Borders, Annual Report 2008: China. http://www.rsf.org/article.php3?id_article=25650

Chapter 5: Economy and Environment

1. 'One Year of My Blood: Exploitation of Migrant Construction Workers in Beijing' http://hrw.org/reports/2008/china0308/

2. 'Labor unrest growing in China: activist', 15 January 2008, Agence France-Presse.

3. ibid.

4. VOA: Officials Report Another Mine Explosion in China, Naomi Martag, 6 December 2007 http://www.china- labour.org.hk/en/node/51547

5. ibid.

6. 'China says developed countries should take lead in fighting climate change', *International Herald Tribune*, 12 March 2008 http://www.iht.com/bin/printfriendly.php?id=10972235

Appendix:

The Real China Before the Olympics

The following is a summary of the petition drawn up and signed by Teng Biao and Hu Jia in 2007:

China promised in 2001 when it won the bid to host the 2008 Olympic Games to improve its human rights record. But has it kept its promise?

Here is the truth: Fang Zhen, an excellent athlete who holds two national records in throwing in China's Special Sport Games is not allowed to take part in the 2008 Paralympics because his legs were crushed by a tank in Tiananmen Square in June 1989. He has become a living testimony of the crackdown.

The Olympic projects have resulted in serious corruption and widespread bribery. Liu Zhihua, Chief Commander of the Olympic constructions and the former deputy mayor of Beijing has been arrested for massive embezzlement.

To clear space for the Olympic constructions, thousands of houses were destroyed without proper compensation. Brothers Ye Guozhu and Ye Guoqiang were imprisoned after they lodged a legal appeal after their house was demolished. Over 1.25 million people are reported to have been forced to move home because of the Olympics. Twenty per cent of the demolished households will fall into poverty.

To polish the image of China's cities, petitioners, beggars and the homeless are being detained or repatriated. Human rights activists, political dissidents, freelance writers and journalists are being persecuted.

Countless websites have been closed and blogs deleted. Sensitive words are filtered out. Many websites hosted abroad are blocked.

Religious freedom is repressed. Torture is common in detention centres, labour camps and prisons. Labour camps allow the police to lock up citizens for up to four years without any trial.

We firmly hold the following belief that there are no real Olympic Games without human rights and dignity. For China and for the Olympics human rights must be honoured.

A Brief Timeline of Modern Chinese History

1911 Wuchang Uprising (10 Oct); Chinese Revolution erupts

1912 Sun Yat-sen officially proclaims the Republic of China (1 Jan) and is inaugurated in Nanjing as the provisional president. Child Emperor Puyi abdicates (12 Feb); Yuan Shih-k'ai emerges as ruler of new republic and is inaugurated as second provisional president in Beijing (10 March); creation of Kuomintang (also known as the KMT or Chinese Nationalist Party)

1916 Beginning of Warlord era

1921 Founding of Communist Party of China (CPC), also known as Chinese Communist Party (CCP)

1927 Chinese Civil War between KMT and CCP (April

1927 until May 1950) goes on intermittently while also fighting the Japanese invaders

1931 Chinese Soviet Republic established in southern Jiangxi province by communist leader Mao Zedong and Zhu De (until 1934)

1934–5 Long March: military retreat by Red armies (forerunner of the People's Liberation Army) to evade Chinese Nationalist Party army, marking the ascent of Mao Zedong

1937 Second Sino-Japanese War (7 July 1937 until 9 Sept 1945)

1949 Founding of People's Republic of China by Mao Zedong. Chinese Nationalist Party retreats to Taiwan

1951 People's Liberation Army defeats Tibetan Army (7 Oct); start of campaign to incorporate Tibet into People's Republic of China

1956 Hundred Flowers campaign, designed to encourage free thinking and provide solutions to state problems

1957 Anti-rightist campaigns, backlash to the Hundred Flowers campaign, persecuting those (especially in the legal sector) with alleged right-wing sympathies

1958 The Great Leap Forward, an economic and social campaign designed to industrialise China (until 1960)

1959 Great Sparrow campaign, a purging of the country's sparrows which leads inadvertently to famine when insects destroy crops

1960 Sino-Soviet split

1962 Sino-Indian War

1964 Destruction of Four Olds campaign to modernise China; publication of *The Little Red Book*, quotations from Chairman Mao

1966–76 Cultural Revolution campaign to rid China of the bourgeoisie and promote class revolution

1967 Christian churches closed

1976 Hua Guofeng becomes chairman after Mao's death (Sept)

1978 Deng Xiaoping becomes leader of Communist Party

1979 One-child policy introduced to alleviate overpopulation

1989 Tiananmen Square protests against state authoritarianism (15 April to 4 June)

1993 Jiang Zemin becomes president

1997 Hong Kong handover, marking transfer of sovereignty from UK to China

1998 Golden Shield online censorship and surveillance project founded, designed to monitor and control Internet communications, beginning in 2003

2002–2003 SARS outbreak

2006 Structural work completed on controversial Three Gorges Dam project

2008 Olympic Games held in China

Further Resources

For additional information on the human rights situation in China, there are plenty of resources at the disposal of the reader. What follows is by no means an exhaustive list but it should help the reader get started on additional research.

International Human Rights

To begin with, there are the major international human rights non-governmental bodies, such as **Amnesty International** and **Human Rights Watch**, each with its own website:
http://www.amnesty.org/ and http://www.hrw.org/
Amnesty issues annual reports on China and other countries. HRW puts out a World Report each year and also issues focused reports, such as one on migrant workers, 'One Year of My Blood'.
http://hrw.org/reports/2008/china0308/

The International Society for Human Rights
(http://www.ishr.org/) and its national branches are independent non-governmental human rights

organisations (NGOs) which base their work on the
Universal Declaration of Human Rights proclaimed by the
United Nations on 10 December 1948. The ISHR seeks
to promote international understanding and tolerance in
all areas of culture and society. It is a non-profit
organisation, independent of all political parties,
governments or religious groups.

Freedom House,
http://www.freedomhouse.org/uploads/
special_report/33.pdf, based in the United States, is
dedicated to promoting free institutions worldwide. It
publishes surveys detailing the state of civil liberties,
political rights and economic freedom around the world
and a Freedom in the World annual survey. It produced
the study 'Speak No Evil: Mass Media Control in
Contemporary China', 2006, a Freedom House Special
Report. http://www.freedomhouse.org/uploads/
special_report/33.pdf

Human Rights Without Frontiers (http://www.hrwf.net/)
is a non-profit organisation based in Brussels that
promotes human rights around the world.

Human Rights in China

Then there are China-specific organisations, in particular, the New York-based group **Human Rights in China** (http://www.hrichina.org/public/index).

There is also the San Francisco-based **Dui Hua Foundation** (http://www.duihua.org/) a non-profit organisation dedicated to advancing the protection of universally recognised human rights in China and in the United States. Human Rights in China published in 2004 the He Qinglian study (http://www.hrichina.org/fs/down loadables/reports/a1_MediaControl1.2004.pdf?revision_id=8992).

There is **Chinese Human Rights Defenders** (CHRD), a non-political, non-governmental network of grassroots and international activists promoting human rights and empowering grassroots activism in China. CHRD's objective is to support human rights activists in China, monitor human rights developments, and assist victims of human rights abuses. CHRD advocates approaches that are non-violent and based on the rule of law. CHRD conducts research, provides information, organises training, supports a programme of small grants to human rights activists and researchers, and offers legal assistance (http://crd-net.org/Article/ShowClass.asp?

ClassID=9). Reports by CHRD include 'Give us back our rights and dignity – 2008: a public letter to the National People's Congress and the Chinese People's Political Consultative Conference by Petitioners' (http://crd-net.org/Article/Class71/200802/20080227212538_7778.html [in Chinese]).

China Labour Bulletin (http://www.china-labour.org.hk/en/) was founded in 1994 by labour activist Han Dongfang and has grown into a proactive outreach organisation that seeks to defend and promote workers' rights in China. It supports the development of democratic trade unions, respect for and enforcement of the country's labour laws and the full participation of workers in the creation of civil society.

The US State Department issues an annual report on the human rights situation in China, including Tibet, Hong Kong and Macau. The most recent one is available at http://www.state.gov/g/drl/rls/hrrpt/2007/100518.htm.

China also issues an annual human rights report on the United States. That one, 'Full Text of Human Rights Record of the United States in 2007', is available at http://www.chinadaily.com.cn/china/2008-03/13/content_6533800.htm.

The Congressional-Executive Commission on China was created by the US Congress in October 2000, with the legislative mandate to monitor human rights and the development of the rule of law in China, and to submit an annual report to the president and the Congress. Its annual report for 2007 is at http://frwebgate.access.gpo.gov/cgi-bin/getdoc.cgi?dbname=110_house_hearings&docid=f:38026.pdf

The United Kingdom government issues a biannual Country of Origin Information Report on the twenty countries that generate the most asylum applications in the UK. The latest report on China is at http://www.homeoffice.gov.uk/rds/pdfs07/china-190107.doc.

Overseas Chinese and Tibetan Organisations

There are also Overseas Chinese organisations, such as the **Independent Federation of Chinese Students and Scholars**, formed in 1989 in Chicago (http://www.ifcss.org/home/) and representing 40,000 Chinese students in the United States. The organisation, which stems from the bloody suppression of the

Tiananmen Square demonstrations of 1989, says it cherishes human rights.

There are also groups devoted to specific issues, such as press freedom, religious freedom, labour rights and Tibet. **The International Campaign for Tibet** (http://www.savetibet.org/) describes its work as promoting human rights and democratic freedoms for the people of Tibet. Its chairman is the Hollywood personality Richard Gere.

The Tibetan government-in-exile's official website is http://www.tibetinfo.net/

Freedom of the Press
Reporters Without Borders
(http://www.rsf.org/rubrique.php3?id_rubrique=20) provides information on many countries regarding freedom of the press and also publishes an annual survey on press freedom around the world.

The Committee to Protect Journalists
(http://www.cpj.org/) is an independent, non-profit organisation dedicated to defending press freedom worldwide. Its report Censorship at Work: The Newsroom in China can be accessed at the following website:

http://www.cpj.org/Briefings/2007/Falling_Short/China/5.
html

Religious Freedom

The US Commission on International Religious Freedom
(http://www.uscirf.gov/) is a US Federal agency created
by the International Religious Freedom Act in 1998 to
monitor the status of freedom of religion around the
world. It designates 'countries of particular concern' for
ongoing, egregious violations of religious freedom and
China is on that list.

The Olympic Games

The Olympic Games have produced NGOs too, including
http://www.olympicwatch.org/,
which describes its mission as being to monitor the
human rights situation in the People's Republic of China
in the run-up to the 2008 Olympic Games and to
campaign to achieve positive change in the lives of the
people of China.